30p

KU-112-195

THE CHINESE
RED ARMY

WITHDRAWN FROM STOCK

WITHDRAWN FROM STOCK

THE CHINESE RED ARMY

CAMPAIGNS AND POLITICS SINCE 1949

GERARD H. CORR

 OSPREY

First published in 1974 by
Osprey Publishing Ltd.,
707 Oxford Road, Reading, Berkshire
© Copyright 1974 Gerard H. Corr
All rights reserved

ISBN 0 85045 162 0

Printed in Great Britain by
Cox & Wyman Ltd, London, Reading and Fakenham

For Mai

Preface

Since the foundation of the Communist regime in Peking in 1949, its military arm, the People's Liberation Army (PLA), has been involved in four conflicts – the invasion of Tibet in 1950 and the later revolt, the Korean War, the 1962 expedition against India, and armed confrontation with the Soviet Union. These campaigns have been widely separated in place and time, but they have a common origin in China's concern for her borders.

During the past hundred years China lost thousands of square miles of territory to the expansionist European powers and from time to time her borders were arbitrarily re-adjusted to suit the needs and purposes of the imperialists. Now she is seeking to recover what she believes to be hers by right. This desire to right past wrongs has little or nothing to do with Communist ideology; rather is it the product of a new nationalism. The Chinese feel deeply the need to show the rest of the world that they have regained their pride and unity and that they have the strength to back their demands.

To rectify her frontiers is for China a part of the working out of her historic destiny – an inevitable process whereby she gains, if not her former position as the centre of a world she once thought her own, then at least a position of equality in power and respect with the other great nations or, as a Chinese would say, civilizations. In this respect the policy of Peking and that of the Nationalists on Taiwan are at one.

It was because China believed she had an evident claim to suzerainty over Tibet that in 1950 she took over that country, which had been given a false sense of independence and security

7

by the British Raj. Twelve years later China went to war with India after a frontier dispute but not simply because of territorial ambition but because a more belligerent India attacked her first. After a short campaign of stunning rapidity the PLA gave up all its hard-won gains and withdrew to its starting-point. More recently, China's border arguments have been with Russia. Here her quarrel is over the unequal treaties imposed on her by the Tsars and subsequently enforced by the Soviet Communists. She seeks redress but does not claim the return of everything taken from her. Russia argues that China is seeking to put the clock back and interfering with the historic process. The two countries are looking down the telescope of history from different ends.

With the Korean War it was somewhat different. The involvement of the Chinese Red Army was brought about by the reckless advance of United Nations forces to the Manchurian border, despite all warnings to stay clear. The newly-established Communist regime felt threatened by America and went into battle to protect itself.

Tibet, Korea, India, Russia have all been reported on and studied in depth by specialists. But it is because they have been treated separately, studied in isolation from one another and sometimes, especially in the case of the Indian War, with a mistaken view of Chinese intentions and policy, that the notion has developed and taken root that China with her enormous army and manpower reserve is an expansionist, aggressive power. A reviewer in the *Journal of the Royal United Services Institute* (December 1972) expressed a widely-held opinion when he wrote: 'The record of Chinese military activity in Korea, Tibet, India and Indo-China, as well as her support of Communist insurgency movements in many parts of the world, reflects an aggressive policy based on military risks.' During the last twenty years this opinion has been bolstered up by steady outpourings of 'Chinese peril' propaganda from America, Russia, Taiwan and other non-Communist Asian states.

Peking has contributed to the ugly picture of China as a bellicose nation by its support of revolutionary movements in Asia, Africa and Latin America. In most cases this support has been expressed in no more than words; but on occasion arms also have been supplied. Too much should not be made of this. China's aid to overseas Communist or left-wing revolutionaries has been infinitesimal compared to that given by the Soviet Union. Even in Vietnam, her contribution to the bloody war on her own doorstep has been in the main confined to civilian goods such as food and clothing, although under a well-defined arrangement some anti-aircraft guns, small arms and engineer troops have been dispatched from time to time. This help to her Communist ally and neighbour has been nothing, of course, compared to that provided by Russia on the one side and America on the other.

Such is the background of the story of the Red Army that I have to tell. To bring the reader up to the year 1949 I have briefly traced the progress of the Army from its foundation onwards to the Civil War of the 'twenties and 'thirties, its war against the Japanese invaders and the civil conflict resumed after 1945. In relating the PLA's story a certain amount of compression has been necessary, and it must be admitted that deduction and interpretation has played a rather bigger part in the assessment of China's political and military strategy than it would have played in the considera-tion of the armed forces of most other nations. With the Chinese this is unavoidable. The limitations placed on non-Chinese students of the Chinese by the Chinese themselves will probably never be removed. Even if entry into China were easier than it is today, the student could have recourse to no Public Records Office to con-sult official documents. This is a handicap under which all obser-vers of, and commentators upon, the Chinese scene have to labour.

My debt is therefore the greater to those scholars who have gone ahead and taken the 'long march' deep into Chinese military and political history; it is their works on the various campaigns and events that are here brought together in one.

The volumes I have found most useful are listed in the biblio-graphy, but I wish to pay tribute to three books upon which I have drawn most heavily. My chapter on the India War has been greatly influenced by the pioneering work of Neville Maxwell. His *India's China War*, published by Jonathan Cape is a basic source book for any who wish to study that campaign further. In his *Defeat in the*

9

Preface

East Michael Elliott-Bateman has made a profound study of Mao Tse-tung's guerrilla strategy and its influence on modern warfare. I am grateful to his publishers, the Oxford University Press, for permission to quote from this book. Mr Dennis Bloodworth, Far East Correspondent of *The Observer*, gives many insights into Chinese military psychology in his *Chinese Looking Glass*, and with his publishers, Secker and Warburg, readily granted me permission to quote.

I have received much encouragement in my writing from my friends in Malaysia and Singapore. In particular I should like to thank Mr Cheah Boon Kheng, of the *Straits Times*, who gave generously of his time and friendship, as did my former colleague, Mr N. S. Mutthana, now deputy editor of *The Statesman of India*.

Many people assisted me in their many ways, but they are not to be held responsible for my conclusions and prejudices. Some may argue that I have presented the Chinese in too favourable a light. To this I reply that those who wish to read of a different China will find no lack of derogatory books, and that in the preparation and writing of my own contribution I have tried wherever possible to view situations, both political and military, as they may have been viewed at the time from Peking. China also has her case. Unfortunately, in presenting it she is more often than not her own worst enemy. The constant lowering of the bamboo curtain has kept her in isolation and has denied to those who are interested opportunities to inquire more closely. Recently, however, China has relaxed towards the rest of the world and her readiness to meet people at least half-way has quickened interest in her affairs. But still a great deal of what is written on China is done by specialists for specialists. Sinologist speaks to Sinologist.

Let me say, then, in conclusion, that my writing is not for the expert. It is for the general reader anxious to gain an overall picture of Chinese military activity during the past twenty-five years. And, for once, the picture is drawn from the Chinese side of the Great Wall.

GERARD H. CORR

Singapore and
Kuala Lumpur, 1973

Contents

List of Illustrations   13
The Chinese Communist Soldier   19
The Crucible: 1927–1949   28
The Campaign in Tibet: 1950–1960   43
The Korean War: 1950–1953   65
War with India: 1962   92
Confrontation with Russia: 1969–1973   112
The Army and Politics   141
The Army for the 'Seventies   158
Bibliography   169
Index   173

List of Illustrations

1. A PLA section on duty at the Great Wall of China, 1937
2. Non-combatant peasants organizing transport of food to the front line
3. A study of a 'Surprise Soldier'
4. The Red Army enters the capital to welcoming crowds
5. Prisoners of Chiang Kai-shek
6. Assault troops practise a beach landing on Hainan Island, April 1950
7. Major General Edward Almond questioning a Chinese prisoner
8. Prisoners captured by the Americans in the Korean War
9. Chinese soldiers captured in North Korea, November 1950
10. A PLA officer briefing a North Korean officer before handing over command
11. PLA soldiers captured by U.S. Marines
12. Chinese soldiers rejoice with North Koreans at the news of their going home
13. PLA men taking their leave of their Korean bunker
14. Lin Piao in the 1950s
15. Lin Piao in his 'regalia' of a Marshal in the PLA
16. A 1951 march-past
17. PLA men supporting Mao's 1958 hard-line approach to Taiwan
18. Tanks and crews on parade in Peking, 1957
19. Light tanks in Peking's 'Red Square'
20. PLA tank crews line up for inspection

List of Illustrations

21. PLA weapons inspection
22. PLA men bringing Mao's Thoughts to the peasants
23. Soldiers on Hainan Island praise Mao
24. A display of force to mark the thirtieth anniversary of the foundation of the Communist Party, 1951
25. Chinese troops marching over the Yingko Pass
26. A jovial Mao Tse-tung
27. Mao with his old friend, the late Edgar Snow
28. Liu Shao-chi and Chou En-lai
29. Chu Teh, Madame Soong Ching-ling, Liu Shao-chi
30. Chu Teh, founding father of the People's Liberation Army
31. Chairman Mao and Defence Minister Lin Piao at a Peking rally during the Cultural Revolution
32. A PLA soldier under instruction
33. The PLA on patrol in Shanghai
34. A PLA battle exercise
35. Mao and Lin receive the acclamation of PLA soldiers
36. A girl soldier, 1972
37. Red soldiers demonstrating their disapproval of Liu Shao-chi in Inner Mongolia
38. New PLA recruits at a between-training chat
39. Border guards on duty, August 1969
40. PLA men guard the Soviet Embassy in Peking
41. A border argument on the frozen Ussuri
42. The Ussuri River and Damansky Island
43. Soviet soldiers receiving a briefing at the Ussuri River, March 1969
44. Militiamen during the mass rally in Kwangchow, March 1969
45. Chinese guards arguing with their Russian counterparts
46. A PLA patrol on the banks of the Amur River
47. The Chinese 'attack' Russians on Damansky Island
48. A border 'demonstration'
49. Russian Army Colonel D. V. Leonov killed on 15 March 1969 on Damansky Island

50. PLA men waiting to go on leave in Canton

51. PLA soldiers on parade at Peking Airport for the arrival of President Nixon, 21 February 1972

52. Keng Yu-chi talking to journalists at Yuang, February 1972

53. Members of the 196th Infantry Division hold up their targets before a shooting exhibition

54. Review order for President Nixon's inspection

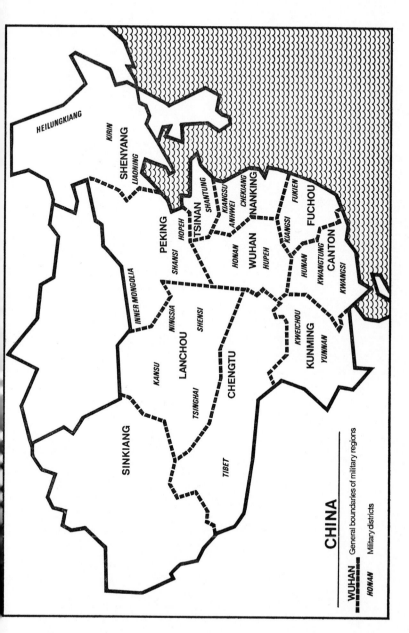

CHINA

WUHAN General boundaries of military regions

HONAN Military districts

B

THE CHINESE
COMMUNIST SOLDIER

Let the Chinese dragon sleep for when
she awakes she will astonish the world

– Napoleon

Western commanders have usually found it difficult to accept that
Asian peasants can be a match for their own men. And this consistent refusal to face realities, having its roots in lingering notions
of racial superiority, has resulted since the turn of the century in a
catalogue of disasters and near-catastrophe for the European and
American armies in the Far East and South-East Asia.

During the Second World War this superior attitude led British
commanders to refuse Chinese offers of help when it could have
been of great assistance. For instance, Chinese aid from the mainland might have prolonged the defence of Hong Kong in 1941 and
inflicted greater hurt on the Japanese. But the offer of a division
from one of Chiang Kai-shek's armies was declined almost con-
temptuously. Similarly in Malaya, efforts to mobilize and train
the local Chinese were for a time actively discouraged, only to be
undertaken when the fate of the Peninsula and Singapore was
sealed. Those Chinese who were admitted into the volunteer infantry companies and the hastily recruited 'Dalforce' fought with
stubborn courage, and it was the Chinese who later formed the
backbone of the anti-Japanese resistance. Yet again, during the
retreat out of Burma, General Alexander declined with obvious
disdain a suggestion of Chinese assistance. He was soon to change
his mind when the British situation continued to deteriorate.

By the time the Korean War came round, the Chinese soldier
still stood low in the estimation of the majority of Westerners.
For this Chiang's Nationalists were in part responsible; during
the war against Japan the Americans had put great faith in the
Generalissimo, only to be severely disillusioned when he spent

19

more energy devising ways of avoiding committing his troops to battle than of furthering the prosecution of the war on the mainland. The poor performance of the Nationalists, first against the Japanese (except in Burma) and then against the Communists, had reinforced the view that Chinese armies, no matter how well supplied and equipped, would always be of relatively poor calibre. What was not properly understood was that the men of the People's Liberation Army were an entirely different breed from those who had filled the Nationalist ranks. The Civil War, both in the 'thirties and on its resumption after 1945, had been reported mainly from the Government's side and the Reds had received scant attention. They were given little credit for defeating their better armed and numerically stronger opponents. After all, one set of Chinese beating another did not count for much.

The level of Chinese military competence was assumed by outsiders to be little above the level at which it had always been – not a very high one. The individual soldier was understood to be courageous and willing in certain circumstances; a number of European commanders who had had to deal with Chinese troops had commented favourably upon their potential. It was 'Vinegar Joe' Stilwell, the American who was himself to command Chinese soldiers in the war against Japan, who put his finger on the weak spot. He reported to Washington in the 1930s that the Chinese soldier was 'excellent material, wasted and betrayed by stupid leadership'. This had been true for a long time; the reason, as with most things Chinese, was to be found in their history.

From earliest times China had developed a tradition of cultivating the arts of peace, diplomacy and compromise rather than those of war. The profession of arms was held in little esteem by government or people – except in times of national emergency. An ancient Taoist maxim ran: 'You do not use good iron to make nails, nor good men to make soldiers', and this summed up the nation's attitude to the military for centuries; indeed, up to the Communists' arrival on the scene. At the same time Buddhists, Confucius and Mencius had preached a gentle philosophy which took deep root in the consciousness of the people. For the Chinese, war developed into a complicated game of manoeuvre, deviousness and trickery, with a heavy reliance on espionage and sub-version. To bring troops to the point of actual physical combat was regarded as being tantamount to a reverse; military operations became almost an art form.

This oblique approach to warfare had nothing to do with physical cowardice or the lack of the will to fight; it emerged gradually as it was realized that there was no such thing as complete victory, a final battle solving all problems. War was seen in the long run to be counter-productive. But if one had to fight then it was better to defeat the enemy by strategic and diplomatic combinations, always with an eye to a possible com-promise, than attempt to annihilate him and leave a legacy of hatred and a desire for revenge among those bound to survive.

A consequence, however, of holding the military in such low regard, was that few men of the right calibre chose to make a career out of the army. There were other avenues open to those with ambition and ability seeking power and wealth. The quality of leadership in wartime was therefore variable, although for-tunately for the Chinese someone of sufficient stature usually emerged to command the armies in the not infrequent times of need.

But army commanders had a thankless task; they knew it, and as a result their loyalty to their men and to the state was as often in doubt as their ability. Fully aware of this, rulers tried to ensure that the generals would give of their best by threatening them with reprisals if they failed in their duty. Thus, Chinese generals were more often than not motivated by the desire to save their own skins. The spear of fear pricked their backs and prodded them on to action, but they were anxious also to avoid defeat and so helped to develop the tradition of protracted manoeuvring. The 'grand old Duke of York' would have been at home in any Chinese army. The system of enforced loyalty flourished until recent times and was exercised by Chiang Kai-shek over some of his more doubtful cohorts.

In times of peace the Chinese were always grateful to see the army fade into obscurity, and by the time the West began to make serious inroads into the country in the 19th century this

21

downgrading of the military had reached such an extent that it was too late to repair the damage caused by neglect. The Europeans won relatively easy victories and suffered more casualties through disease than through battle.

Because of economic pressures the Communists from time to time have been forced to ignore this lesson of history, and on a few occasions the PLA has been reduced to little more than a 'land army', the soldiers tilling the soil or engaging in engineering and construction work. This has caused dissension in the top ranks, particularly among those who have advocated a more conventional and professional military system. But in bowing to the necessity of sending hundreds of thousands of men to the countryside to help with the planting and harvesting, the Red leaders have also taken advantage of the situation to remind the men of their heritage, the land, and the continuing need for its defence against the 'imperialists, foreign devils, and their running dogs [jackals]'. This harping on the soldier's heritage, 'the good earth', produces a ready response, for the vast majority of the men in the Red Army come, like their forefathers, from the land.

In pre-Communist days the peasant was known as 'Old Hundred Names', a nickname referring to the mythical 'one hundred families' who founded China. By giving him this title the authorities allowed the lowest serf a claim to aristocratic lineage. It was about all he was entitled to. Worked almost to death, cruelly taxed, subsisting on a near-starvation diet, his life and death resting on the whim of a landlord, the peasant learned fortitude, the stoical acceptance of his lot; fatalism was ingrained in his character. Yet somehow he managed to retain a sense of humour and a ready cheerfulness. When he was recruited or drafted into the army, the characteristics which kept him alive in his village helped him to survive in uniform. But since after all he had not much to fight for, his conduct in battle was usually unpredictable. He was apt to run away at the sound of the guns, to desert when he had the chance, to join the other side if it looked like winning; and yet there were times when he would fight with matchless courage and tenacity. Dennis Bloodworth in his analysis of

Chinese psychology, *Chinese Looking Glass*, explains this contradiction in behaviour, with its 'extremes of apparent cowardice and self-sacrifice, pacifism and aggressiveness' as follows: 'A Chinese will not . . . throw away his life profitlessly in a pointless battle joined on badly-chosen terrain for an inferior cause. But if the time comes when he can sell it at a price worth dying for, he sells. And that, to him, is the measure of valour.'

In fighting the Japanese invaders in the 'thirties, whether under the Red or the Nationalist flag, the Chinese peasants saw a cause worth fighting and dying for; and die they did, millions of them, in a series of battles of a scale equal to those in Flanders in the First World War or on the Russian front in the Second. In the defence of Shanghai alone the Nationalists sustained a quarter of a million casualties.

'Old Hundred Names' who joined up with the Communists rather than the Nationalists had another dream besides that of a land cleared of the detested Japanese: a country free of the bondage in which it had been held for hundreds of years. In the 1920s and 1930s the Chinese were stretched on a rack tightened continually by landlords, the cogs greased by the slippery hands of corrupt officials and turned by rapacious foreign governments and international business houses. Everywhere there was poverty and disease; famine and flood regularly visited the land and took their toll in millions of lives. Could this appalling, endless tapestry of life, stitched over the centuries in human misery and degradation, threaded by successive inefficient and uncaring emperors and governments, ever be torn apart? Many had tried, failed and died in the attempt. Could the Communists do better?

Mao Tse-tung and his fellow revolutionaries believed they could; there was nothing that the beleaguered peasantry could not achieve if properly mobilized, given strong leadership by example and inspiration arising from proved success. They brought into being a new army, a new type of soldier. To the peasants in the past, armies had meant plunder, murder, looting, devastation of land and crops, young men conscripted from the fields at the point of the bayonet; wives and daughters taken away, never to be seen or heard from again. But the behaviour of

23

the Red troops was totally different. 'Old Hundred Names' had never seen anything quite like it. It was a revelation. The Red soldiers laid aside their arms and assisted in the fields; they paid for their food; they were courteous and kind; they kicked out the oppressive landlords and distributed the land fairly; wives and young women were safe in their company; they even gave rudimentary lessons in reading and writing; but above all they fought – and sometimes they won.

The peasant, even though with hundreds of years of cynicism behind him, was impressed; the new doctrine appealed to him. More important, it was acceptable since it slotted into the framework of Chinese life and thought (an early example of the pragmatism of Mao); certainly it was authoritarian, but even that was traditional since all previous Chinese systems of government had been based on a strong, central core. The peasant saw in the Communist ideals a way of ridding the country of the locusts, native and foreign, who lived off the fat of the land, the fat which he himself had produced by labour from dawn to dusk; he saw a way of life fit for a Chinese, in which dignity and harmony could be recovered, possibly even peace and prosperity. 'Old Hundred Names' liked what he saw; he decided to fight for it. Later, after victory, he wasn't so sure he had been right – Mao's approach had been such as to offer everyone something. But then it was too late. Anyway, that was his grandson's problem.

For those who volunteered, those who decided to wear the Red star, Mao laid down a whole series of rules and principles for behaviour and conduct. The most important were: orders must be obeyed at all times, nothing must be confiscated from the poor, and anything taken from landlords must be handed over to the Communist authorities. Another code of conduct was made into a song. Among its maxims were the following: be courteous and polite to the people, and help them at all times; replace all damaged articles and return borrowed ones; pay for everything you get and be honest in all transactions; be sanitary and build latrines at a safe distance from people's houses.

The most famous of Mao's teachings were his four principles for the waging of guerrilla warfare:

When the enemy advances, we retreat.
When the enemy halts and encamps, we trouble him.
When the enemy seeks to avoid battle, we attack.
When the enemy retreats, we pursue.

These slogans were repeated endlessly until every recruit could say them by heart – and, more important, until they were thoroughly understood. Mao's regulations, his orders of the day, may sound prosaic today, but it must be remembered that the Communist leaders were dealing for the most part with illiterate peasants who needed to be told in the simplest way possible what was expected of them, and how they should go about their duties. Mao and his aides had not only to teach their recruits how to soldier (and the toughest soldiering of all – partisan fighting, which calls on all the individual's reserves of stamina and courage over long periods), but also to educate them even in such basics as hygiene and self-discipline. The simplicity of Mao's teachings has been sneered at, his reputation therefore as a strategist and tactician derided. But this is because the difficulties of training a peasant army under the constant pressure of wartime conditions are not understood. The evidence of the Red commanders' success in moulding their raw material into disciplined and effective soldiers lies in the history of the struggle and ultimate achievement of the PLA.

Furthermore, Mao's manual of military training differed from all previous practice in the great emphasis placed on the need for careful selection and intensive training of junior leaders. Officers and N.C.O.s were encouraged to act on their own initiative and were drilled in the necessity of paying attention at all times to the well-being of their men. The junior cadres, composed of men of proven ability, highly motivated and with a sense of responsibility to their duties hitherto unknown in Chinese armies, were the brains and muscle upon which the senior commanders came increasingly to rely.

The men who fill the ranks of the PLA today are in many respects similar to its founders. Most of them still come from the land and they retain all the peasant's virtues and vices. They are physically tough with a natural aptitude for infantry soldiering; they have a quick, intuitive intelligence without being over-endowed with imagination; in adversity they are cheerful and self-reliant; they are suspicious by nature, particularly of foreigners, and this can always be whipped into a particular hatred at the will of their political masters; they are fascinated by technical innovation and readily adaptable to what engages their interest; they make exuberant artillerymen. But despite all the efforts made to raise their standard of learning, many of them still cling to superstitious beliefs, the animism they picked up as children in their villages.

But today the average soldier comes from a more stable and healthy background than the recruit of thirty or forty years ago. He is physically better developed, he is less prone to the illnesses and diseases that once ravaged China, and he has at least a rudimentary education. He is of course versed in Mao's thoughts, although not indoctrinated to the extent that is sometimes imagined outside China. He is fiercely patriotic but, like those who have gone before him, he has to be led rather than driven. During the Cultural Revolution ranks were abolished in the PLA, but this does not seem to have impaired discipline, although how the Army manages to function effectively remains something of a mystery.*

Those who don the drab green uniform, both men and women, are probably the most enthusiastic and willing recruits to any army in the world today. Families regard it as a high honour to have a son or daughter in the PLA and children are deliberately encouraged to join up.

The popularity of the Army as a career has nothing to do with the material benefits it offers; these are poor by Western stand-

---

* Derek Davies, who visited China in April, 1973, and wrote an amusing guide to distinguishing officers from the men (*Far East Economic Review*, 23 April 1973) said that the number of breast pockets on a tunic and the number of ball-point pens in them was a good indication to importance; and the cut of the uniform the best clue of all. He concluded: 'Fortunately for discipline, the soldiers themselves apparently have no difficulty in according those in authority the proper degree of respect and obedience.'

ards, and even by those of other Asian countries. Wages are very small, and leave is given only when there is sickness in a soldier's family and his presence is needed at home. Soldiering is very much a full-time occupation; its attraction for young men and women is difficult to define, but there does seem to exist among them a genuine desire to serve the nation in an 'organization' – the PLA sometimes exhibits the traits as much of a vast corporation as of an army – which has a hallowed place in the history of Chinese revolutionary warfare.

Mao's principles for the waging of war and for personal conduct, which were the bedrock upon which the PLA was founded, are still taught and form part of the living tradition of the Army. They have helped to turn peasants into some of the most formidable soldiers the world has seen, soldiers whose ability and courage surprised the U.N. forces in Korea, who ten years later produced a lightning victory against the Indians, and who today disturb Soviet Russia and give the West an occasional shudder at the thought of a 'yellow tide' flooding out of China into the rest of Asia and southward to Australia. The smirks of a generation ago have given place to a respect for Chinese military potential, but the role, the capacity and the aims of the PLA are still widely misinterpreted. These will be examined later; suffice it to say here that although the Army has not been in action since 1962, except for border skirmishing with Soviet troops, there is no reason to doubt that the Chinese soldier will fight, if called upon to do so, no less courageously and effectively than the original founder of his many regiments, 'Old Hundred Names'.

THE CRUCIBLE: 1927-1949

The object of war is to preserve oneself and
annihilate the enemy – *Mao Tse-tung*

Our soldiers join the Army to serve the
people, not the officers – *Chu Teh*

The Red Army was born out of a mutiny. On 1 August 1927*,
units of the 24th Division of the Nationalist Eleventh Army
stationed near Nanchang, capital of the southern province of
Kiangsi, rose against the leadership of Chiang Kai-shek and the
High Command of the Kuomintang (National People's Party)
Armed Forces. One of the organizers of the mutiny was a 40-
year-old general, Chu Teh, an unusual man and one with an
unlikely background for a Chinese Communist. Born of rich
land-owners, Chu Teh received a good traditional education and
then went on to study at a military academy before joining the
Republican Army of Dr Sun Yat-sen. He rose to the rank of
brigadier, and then obtained a high civil appointment in Yunnan
Province; but his duties were light and with time on his hands
he became a victim of the opium-smoking habit.

Chu Teh was a cultured man, well-versed in the classics but
with catholic reading tastes, and his mind was restless. His
horizons stretched beyond the frontiers of his duties, and he came
to realize that his easy official life and his addiction to opium
would eventually deaden all energy and ambition. In an early
display of strength of will and purpose, Chu Teh – the name, in-
cidentally, means 'red virtue' – decided to cut loose from everything which bound him. Leaving his wife and family, he boarded
a liner bound for Europe and virtually imprisoned himself in his
cabin. On the long voyage he suffered the agonies of drug withdrawal, but by the time his ship docked in France he had cured

---

* Some authorities put the mutiny date at 31 July, but 1 August is 'official'
and generally accepted.

himself. He moved around Europe and eventually reached Moscow where he attended the congress of the Toilers of the East and spent some time studying Marxism and furthering his military knowledge. He returned to China in 1925 a committed Communist.

Party contacts in Shanghai managed to obtain for him an appointment as commander of the Nanchang provincial forces – not a difficult matter at that time since the Reds were in uneasy alliance with the Kuomintang and men with military ability were in demand. On taking up his post Chu Teh came into contact with a junior officer of the 24th Division by the name of Lin Piao ('Tiger cat' Lin), an intense, sickly-looking man who shared his political philosophy. Lin was a product of the famous Whampoa Military Academy in Canton when its commandant was Chiang Kai-shek and Chou En-lai its political officer.

Chu Teh, Lin Piao and other like-minded officers instigated the Nanchang mutiny after the Kuomintang's sudden repudiation of the Red alliance and the purge and massacre of Communists in Shanghai and other cities and ports. But the uprising was mishandled. Strong elements of the 24th Division refused to 'go over' and when reinforcements from the Eleventh and Twentieth Armies arrived on the scene the mutineers were driven out of Nanchang. Chu Teh gathered together the survivors of his original force of about 10,000 and retreated southward into Kwangtung Province. This region failed to prove either a safe haven or a base for revolution and after much aimless wandering he made contact with another struggling revolutionary, Mao Tse-tung, and in the spring of 1928 the Nanchang remnants joined up with Mao's force in the mountainous region on the Hunan/Kiangsi border.

This link-up of two weary and battered armies is now regarded as one of the great milestones in the progress of the Communist revolution and is celebrated in song, poetry and epic painting. It was a formative event and out of it came the First Workers' and Peasants' Army, as the PLA was originally called. The Reds, however, have chosen to celebrate the Army's anniversary on the date of the failed mutiny. Chu Teh, who later became commander-in-chief of the PLA, is justly honoured as its founding father, while Lin Piao's subsequent rise to power in the political and military hierarchy was undoubtedly due in part to this early connection with Mao and Chu Teh; he had been in at the very beginning.

In May 1928, the motley collection of ex-Nationalist soldiers, half-trained peasants and eager helpers, which constituted the Communist forces hardly deserved to be described as an army. They were the survivors and refugees of dozens of major and minor rebellions against Chiang up and down the country. They came together at a time when the fortunes of the Reds had reached their nadir. They were a rabble with little hope of surviving a well-conducted and determined sweep against them. But the General-issimo delayed. He held his hand; and it was to cost him dearly in the years to come.

But to the outside world Chiang appeared at this time to be the strong man China needed. When he assumed the mantle of Dr Sun Yat-sen in 1925 it seemed that destiny had selected him as the man who would bring to fulfilment a social revolution which had its origins in the Taiping Rebellion of the last century. That had been a peasant-based movement which attempted not only to bring down the Manchu dynasty but also to usher in a pro-gramme of social and agrarian reform. It failed, but it planted a slow burning fuse among the people and in 1911 touched off another explosion of frustration and anger which finally demol-ished the Manchu throne. A republic was established, but Dr Sun, its first President, was never able to establish his authority over the country and China became a prey to warlord rivalry and intensified foreign exploitation. When Dr Sun died of cancer, Chiang Kai-shek, his adviser on military affairs, took over the Kuomintang leadership and decided to act boldly and directly to enforce his Party's control.

From his southern base Chiang set out northward on an expedition intended to drive out the warlords, re-unite the people and define his own authority for restoring the nation's affairs to some sort of order. The peasants rallied to Chiang's cause; they joined his armies, helped to feed them, assisted their passage through the countryside by bringing in intelligence and attacking warlord supporters and landlords. In the cities the worker turned on their employers, striking and rioting, and attacked those foreigners, particularly missionaries, who could not call on European or American troops to defend their compounds and businesses.

Chiang's progress was triumphant. But as revolution spread he became alarmed. His predecessor had formed the alliance with the Reds only two years before Sun's death and at a time when he was depressed by his failures. Sun had decided to break completely with the past; if the fledgling Communist Party, tied inevitably with Russia, could help to forge a new China within the framework of the Kuomintang ideals, well and good. But Chiang was unhappy at being harnessed with the Reds. Their programme was far too extreme for his liking. He was suspicious of their intentions and his doubts seemed confirmed as trouble erupted throughout the country during his northward march. Chiang, in many ways an old-style ruler dressed in modern uniform, was alarmed that both local and foreign support for his movement might be withheld because of the excesses perpetrated in the name of the Kuomintang. The right wing of his party protested at a reform programme which placed the interests of workers and peasants before those of employers and landowners, while Western governments and business houses grew apprehensive for their concessions and their huge stake in the Chinese economy. They accused the Kuomintang of being a Communist-front organization. Chiang decided that, if his government were to survive, he needed their backing and their money. Suddenly, he turned on the Communists.

In Shanghai, were Chou En-lai was busy organizing a general strike, Chiang let loose troops, underworld gangsters and secret-society thugs, on Reds, union leaders, and any suspected of association with either. China's biggest and richest city was gripped by a reign of terror. Thousands were gunned down by firing squads, murdered in the streets and in their very homes. Throughout 1927, similar massacres were carried out in other cities in a determined attempt to exterminate the Reds and their sympathizers at one blow. The Communist Party was banned and membership of it declared a crime punishable by death. Sun Yat-sen's widow, appalled at the turn of events, went into exile along with many other supporters of his ideals.

The Communists of course retaliated. Landlords were murdered, employers were executed, riots swept through many cities and, as at Nanchang, army units mutinied. But the Reds had nothing like the strength of the Kuomintang, which in most places quickly got the upper hand. Chou En-lai was captured in Shanghai but managed to escape. He made his way to join Mao Tse-tung, who had also survived his disastrous Autumn Harvest Rising in Hunan.

By 1928 Chiang seemed to be master of China. His government was recognized by overseas powers delighted with the assurances they had received about their interests; foreign banks were generous with their loans; the warlord problem was largely resolved; and the surviving Reds had gone underground or were hiding out in the countryside. This was Chiang's opportunity; it was his great chance to consolidate his hold over the country through reform and enlightened rule. He let the opportunity slip; repressive measures were continued against peasants and industrial workers, corruption spread everywhere, and nothing was done to ease the stranglehold of foreigners upon the economy. Chiang reserved to himself dictatorial powers but did nothing to remove the underlying causes of China's weakness. For two years Mao's forces in Kiangsi were left to their own devices.

The Reds took full advantage of this lull and extended their mini-state within a state to form a Soviet in which peasants ruled themselves through elected councils, shared the work on the land and underwent military training. But neither were they without their troubles. The Party was still Moscow-oriented and many wanted to follow the orthodox line of promoting revolution through the working class, by capturing cities, towns and ports. It was by following this dogma that the Reds had been nearly wiped out in Shanghai and Canton, and Mao realized that the conditions for this type of revolution did not exist in an underdeveloped, largely rural China. He began to propound the theory of holding the countryside and isolating the towns, fighting a mobile guerrilla war rather than engaging in costly pitched battles. He argued cogently that a revolutionary army must be established on a broad territorial base, with people and soldiers sharing all the tasks, consolidated in their aims and outlook. This was near-heresy to the Moscow-trained elite who still dominated the Party's central executive and issued directives from their Shanghai hide-out.

The crunch between the opposing sides in this internal ideological argument came in 1930. By this time the Kiangsi Soviet was the centre base for fifteen liberated areas and the Red Army had a regular strength of 60,000 men, plus the active support of hundreds of thousands of peasants. Chu Teh, who had been responsible for training the recruits and welding the various units into an effective army, was ordered to attack Changsha, the capital of Hunan Province. He did so in July. The assault was initially successful, but after ten days of hanging on to the city the Communist casualties became too heavy and Chu Teh had to withdraw. This reverse convince Mao that the Party leaders did not know what they were talking about and that his own doctrine was sound. Guerrilla warfare became the order of the day.

Chu Teh's abortive foray into Hunan also served to infuriate Chiang Kai-shek who had been distracted by quarrels within the Kuomintang and a fresh outbreak of trouble from the warlords. Early in December he launched the first of his 'bandit extermination' campaigns. Mao's new tactics now paid off; the Kiangsi Soviet soldiers melted away before Nationalist attacks, struck where least expected, and cut off communications and supplies. A bewildered and exhausted Nationalist army went on to the defensive and after suffering heavy losses retreated a safe distance from the roving, hard-hitting Reds.

This unexpected setback convinced Chiang that the Communists presented a real threat to his regime. He insisted publicly that he was fighting 'bandit gangs', but his new preparations to clear out Kiangsi revealed how seriously he now regarded the Red Army. In February 1931, he embarked on another campaign – with the same result. Undeterred, he gathered together an even greater force and let loose a third campaign in July. The

C

Reds manoeuvred as before, but this time they were enticed into fighting a pitched battle and bloodily repulsed a heavy assault at Kaohsing. This defeat and the news that the Japanese had seized Manchuria persuaded Chiang to call off the campaign.

After appeasing the Japanese in the north – a policy which disgusted many Chinese and created further disillusionment with the Kuomintang – Chiang returned to what he regarded as China's major problem, the Communists in Kiangsi. He mustered an army of a quarter of a million men, but after some early successes this campaign also ended in failure. But the Generalissimo was nothing if not stubborn, and he determined on another, 'final' operation. He engaged the services of a number of German officers – in doing so he convinced many that he was fast becoming a Fascist – who proposed a strategy of surrounding the Soviet, hemming it in with blockhouses, slowly strangling it and then trampling it down with an avalanche offensive. The campaign opened in October 1933, and was to result in one of the great epics of modern military history – the Long March.

The Party Central Executive had by this time moved to Kiangsi from Shanghai and so exercised greater control over their subordinate, Mao. It was decided to revert to the old policy of fighting pitched battles in defence of territory. This played into the hands of the Nationalist strategy and was to have catastrophic results for the Red Army. Within a year it had suffered 100,000 casualties. Defeat and complete disintegration threatened. In October 1934, the Central Executive handed over to Mao full control of the shattered remnants of the Army and he immediately decided on the only course open if anything was to be saved from the disaster – the abandonment of Kiangsi and a break-out from the steel and concrete trap in which the Reds had so obligingly remained for a year.

On 16 October Mao launched a two-pronged attack. The Reds hit hard and fast, fighting in the manner they knew best. An expanding hole was punched through the Nationalist lines and through it poured soldiers, peasants, women and children, baggage columns, supply carts, everything and anything which could be moved or carried. The Long March had begun. The destination was Shensi Province in a remote area of north-west China. This March, an historic feat of human endurance, was to take a whole year, during which the Red columns covered some 8000 miles of territory, crossing eighteen mountain ranges and fording thirty rivers. The route took them through twelve provinces; it has been estimated that not a day passed without a skirmish, beside fifteen major battles fought and won.

The Reds were rarely free from air attack and long-range artillery fire, as Chiang sought to contain them and reduce their numbers. But they kept going, and time and again out-manoeuvred their pursuers. Whether in snow-capped mountains, wet grasslands or swamp, they never marched less than thirty miles a day. They had to contend with harrying Nationalists, warlord forces, hostile tribesmen and aborigine warriors. They died in battle, they died of disease and cold, they suffered tortures from extremes of climate, they died of starvation and they died of exhaustion, they disappeared in treacherous marshes, in rivers and snows, some lost heart and dropped out to die, a few, a very few, gave themselves up.

On 20 October 1935, Mao led his ragged army into Shensi. It was all over. They had come through. Chiang Kai-shek claimed a great victory.

There were good strategical reasons for the Red leaders choosing Shensi as their final destination. It was an area which offered a natural defensive position against any future operations attempted by Chiang; but if it became untenable then the Mongolian border was within easy reach, and if the worst came to the worst, the Soviet Union was not too far away. At the same time the base was ideally situated for offensive moves against north China and the industrially rich Manchuria.

The Army set up its headquarters in Yenan, and a city was established in the caves of a great cliff-face. Some 20,000 people lived in these deep caverns, which proved ideal as shelters from bombing raids. An academy of higher learning and a military academy were organized; hospitals, schools and theatres were established. Yenan became a self-contained Soviet, a colony of moles, reasonably secure from further interference from the Kuomintang.

For eleven years the Red Army was to have its top command housed in hillside caves, and in these caves Mao developed his political and military ideas, destined to shape the future not only of China but of other Asian countries.

By the time the Long March ended the Japanese threat was again looming large. The Reds had made a formal declaration of war against Japan from the Kiangsi Soviet in 1932 – without, of course, being able to do anything about it. And in 1935, before the March was completed, they issued a call for a united front against Japan which was continuing to make inroads on China. Chiang, as much a patriot as any Communist, had continued to lose support because of his appeasement policy, but he argued that his first duty was to rid China of the Communists and that the Japanese could be tackled only when the country was united under the Kuomintang and strong enough to face the aggressor. In his heart he doubted whether China would ever be able to take on the armed might of Japan without outside assistance. But whatever his doubts, the matter was settled once for all in December 1936. Nationalist units in Shensi had become restless at fighting their fellow countrymen rather than the Nippon plunderers. Chiang flew to Sian, the capital of the province, to deal with the trouble. On arrival there he was promptly arrested by a group of officers led by General Chang Hsüeh-liang. He saved himself from being shot by agreeing to an armistice with the Reds and forming a united front with them against the Japanese. Mao and Chou En-lai – the latter negotiated the alliance – accepted that a common front was inconceivable without Chiang to head it; only under Chiang, such was still his standing at home and abroad, could the many and diverse political factions be welded into a patriotic whole.

The agreement having been made, Chiang was released unconditionally. Chang Hsüeh-liang returned voluntarily to the Nationalist capital of Nanking to face a court martial for insubordination. He was too trusting. Chiang has kept him in detention ever since, even moving him under guard to Taiwan when the Kuomintang fell in 1949.

The Sian Incident, as it came to be known, had long-term repercussions for China. Chiang's prestige was given an enormous boost when it was learned that the Communists had agreed to recognize his leadership and authority, and there was a new wave of patriotism and nationalist feeling. The agreement meant that in future China would face Japan as a united nation, and both parties adhered to it for some years because it suited their separate interests.

Events at Sian were not lost on the Japanese military leaders. A united China was the last thing they desired; they feared the new Chinese potential and they decided to strike first. On 7 July 1937, a shooting incident was contrived at the Marco Polo Bridge on the outskirts of Peking. The Japanese used this as a pretext to invade and they quickly overran most of northern China.

The Nationalist Government was eventually forced to retreat behind the mountain barrier of South-West China and Chiang set up a new capital at Chungking, a city on the upper reaches of the Yangtze. To all intents and purposes the Nationalist struggle against the invader was over by 1939. As the Second World War spread from Europe to the Pacific, China's conflict became part of the international struggle. America saw China as a major and vital cog in the war machine to crush Japan, and was desperate to keep her in the struggle. Massive quantities of supplies and equipment were sent to Chiang either along the Burma Road or by airlift over the Himalayas.

But by now Chiang had reverted to his old ideas. He realized that with or without his help, America would defeat Japan. What of China then? He would still have to deal with the Communists. With this in mind he embarked on a policy designed to keep up the flow of American aid but to use as little of it as possible against the enemy. Throughout the war he was long on promises but short on action, content to sit tight in Chungking and prepare for the day of reckoning with Mao and his 'bandits'. The truce with the Communists gradually became a dead letter, attacks were made on them at any opportunity, and for a time Yenan was blockaded.

Despite great provocation Mao and his colleagues had to keep up the pretence of working with the Kuomintang. They needed the war since it gave them an avenue of appeal to the people and put them in a good contrasting light to the Kuomintang. They also feared lest Chiang might one day do a deal with the Japanese, the inevitable result of which would be a joint campaign against themselves. So the Reds continued to prosecute the war as best they could, learned from their mistakes and reverses and went on recruiting soldiers and supporters. They also were preparing, and preparing more realistically, for the showdown with Chiang, whose military inaction was having a disastrous effect on his armies. Sickness, malnutrition, enforced conscription, brutal discipline, corruption and boredom were all helping to reduce morale, fighting efficiency and confidence to a dangerously low state.

When the Japanese war ended abruptly in August 1945 with the atom-bombing of Hiroshima and Nagasaki, both Mao and Chiang were taken by surprise. They had expected it to continue for at least another year and they both believed that America would mount a large-scale invasion of China, probably in the Shanghai area, to clear out the occupying forces. Chiang looked forward to this, since he thought it would assist him in his plans to re-assert full Kuomintang control.

The sudden collapse of Japan left China up for the takers, the most important prize to be won being the industrially developed Manchuria which the Russians, late comers into the Japanese conflict, had swiftly occupied. Mao was first off the mark from his well-placed Shensi base and quickly got his troops to Manchuria. The Nationalist forces moved in at a slower and more cautious rate.

Chiang has since been criticized for even attempting to gain control of Manchuria without first securing his rear by winning absolute control of central China. But Chiang realized not only the strategic importance of the area but also the political necessity of controlling it. If the Communists were allowed to secure it,

MILITARY ORGANISATION OF THE PEOPLE'S REPUBLIC OF CHINA

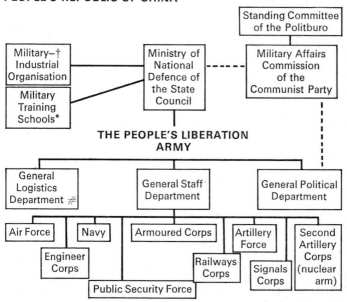

† The military-industrial complex is run by the National Defence Scientific and Technological Commission which supervises research and development into weaponry. The armaments industry is looked after by the National Defence Industrial Staff Office of the State Council.

This Department has replaced the General Rear Services Department. Its many responsibilities include ordnance and finance.

* Although military training schools are the direct concern of the Ministry of National Defence, the running of them is organised by the General Staff Department.

Commanders:		
	Artillery Force	Chang Ta-chih
	Engineer Corps	Chen Shih-chu
	Railway Corps	Chang I-hsiang
	Navy	Hsiao Ching-kuan
	Public Security	Wu Lieh

The service arms are still undergoing a shake-up of senior officers following the downfall of Lin Piao, and the commanders of the Air Force, Armoured Corps, Signals and Second Artillery (Nuclear) have not yet come to light.

REGIONAL ORGANISATION OF THE PEOPLE'S LIBERATION ARMY

(11 Military Regions and 24 Military Districts)

CANTON MR
Commander: Ting Sheng
Commissar: Jen Szu-chung
— HUNAN MD
— KWANGTUNG MD
— KWANGSI MD

CHENGTU MR
Commander: Liang Hsing-chu
Commissar: Li Ta-chang
— TIBET MD

FUCHOU MR
Commander: Han Hsien-chu
Commissar: Chou Chih-ping
— FUKIEN MD — KIANGSI MD

KUNMING MR
Commander: Wang Pi-cheng
Commissar: Chou Hsing
— KWEICHOU MD — YUNNAN MD

LANCHOU MR
Commander:
Commissar: Hsien Heng-han
— KANSU MD — SHENSI MD
— NINGSIA MD — TSINGHAI MD

NANKING MR
Commander: Hsu Shih-yu
Commissar: Chang Chun-chiao
— CHEKIANG MD
— ANHWEI MD
— KIANGSU MD

PEKING MR
Commander: Cheng Wei-shan
Commissar:
— HOPEH MD
INNER MONGOLIA MD
— SHANSI MD

SHENYANG MR
Commander: Chen Hsi-lien
Commissar: Tseng Shao-shan
— KIRIN MD
— HEILUNGKIANG MD
— LIAONING MD

SINKIANG MR
Commander: Lung Shu-chin
Commissar: Tsao Szu-ming

TSINAN MR
Commander: Yang Te-chih
Commissar:
— SHANTUNG MD

WUHAN MR
Commander: Tseng Szu-yu
Commissar: Wang Liu-sheng
— HONAN MD — HUPEH MD

they would be able to set up a separate republic and pose a perpetual threat to the rest of China. Chiang, for once, had read the Communist strategy aright. Whoever ruled Manchuria would eventually rule China. It was to be the central cauldron in which the renewed civil war boiled up between 1946 and 1949.

The months immediately after the Japanese surrender were months of confusion and uncertainty for China, with spasmodic outbreaks of fighting between the Reds and the Kuomintang. The Americans made great efforts to prevent the impending war but greatly annoyed the Communists by continuing to send lavish supplies to the Nationalist forces. Meanwhile, as the months of tension slipped by, the Russians pulled out of Manchuria, and in their turn annoyed the Communists by taking with them valuable industrial plant. The gathering PLA filled the vacuum in the Manchurian countryside, and was ready for action when, in June 1946, China was once again plunged into civil war, both parties being unable to reconcile their profound differences.

For the first eighteen months the military advantage ebbed and flowed, and at the end of 1947 Chiang appeared to have the upper hand. He was still ruler, nominally at least, in most provinces and had control of all the major cities; his forces were twice the size of the PLA and he had absolute control of the air; he was abundantly supplied with arms and ammunition, whereas the Reds, as usual, were forced to rely on what they could capture on the battlefield.

But Chiang's domination, both military and politically, was an illusion. In the nation's eyes he and his faction were discredited for their political and economic mismanagement; corruption in the Army and the civil service had reached staggering proportions; inflation was rampant; the soldiers were ill-fed, poorly disciplined, rarely and badly paid; their performance was increasingly uncertain when up against the tough, battle-hardened Reds.

The year 1948 was decisive in the struggle for supremacy. So far Mao had been content to fight guerrilla warfare, but now, his armies grown to many times their original size with recruits and Nationalist deserters and now well supplied with captured arms, he moved on to mobile warfare and moreover began to accept pitched battles when the balance of advantage seemed in his favour. The tempo of the war was savagely accelerated.

The strength of the Reds advanced with the year. By June they matched the Nationalist forces in both men and equipment. The abandoned battlefields were still the PLA's main source of supply for weaponry, particularly heavy artillery, but the Soviet Union also weighed in and handed over some of the heavy guns they had captured from the Japanese. Deprived of artillery for years, the Reds took to their new prizes with enthusiasm and quickly mastered the techniques of using them.

November saw the surrender of the city of Mukden, the last Nationalist stronghold in Manchuria. Chiang's commanders had, as usual, allowed themselves to be surrounded and then squeezed into capitulation. PLA units were now hastily sent south to engage in the developing battle of Huai Hai. Here, on the plain of Hsuchang, four Nationalist armies had been trapped and immobilized. They totalled 340,000 men, a figure swelled by a further 120,000 when a relieving force broke through only to end bottled up with the others. In one of the greatest battles of modern times, the Red Army executed a classical encircling movement as a preliminary to destroying the enemy piecemeal. For two months the struggle raged, but on 10 January 1949, the inevitable happened, when, with all their supply and communication routes effectively blocked, the Nationalists surrendered. The Red generals claimed to have taken 325,000 prisoners.

This victory opened the gate to central and southern China. Peking was taken without a fight and in the spring 750,000 Red soldiers crossed the Yangtze to begin their triumphal procession across China. In the twelve months from November 1948, they marched 2000 miles, from Mukden to Canton and Chengtu. The Kuomintang collapsed, eaten away by the termites of military incompetence and governmental incapacity. Chiang fled to Taiwan. On 1 October 1949, Chairman Mao Tse-tung formally proclaimed the establishment of the People's Republic. China's dark night was over, and the dawn of a new order was breaking.

'The Chinese people, one quarter of the human race, have now stood up', declared Mao.

THE CAMPAIGN IN TIBET: 1950-1960

If my people had been able to follow
[the policy of non-violence] with me, the condition
of Tibet would at least have been
somewhat better now than it is – *The Dalai Lama*

A stone added to a roadside cairn was once the traditional way in which the traveller to Tibet registered his safe arrival on 'the roof of the world'. In the late autumn of 1950 forces of the Chinese People's Liberation Army heralded their unwanted presence on Tibetan soil in a different but no less curious manner. They banged gongs and sounded bugles while a cacophony of propaganda was let loose over Peking radio. The explanation for this unusual approach to battle lay in China's attitude towards Tibet. The Communists saw themselves in the role of liberators of an oppressed people confined to the dark ages and held there by a feudal and theocratic state. They were genuine in their desire of wanting to take the country back within China's frontiers through peaceful means. It was hoped that intensive propaganda would undermine the Tibetan Government's will to resist and that the deliberate noise created by the advance units would scare away the Tibetan forces sent to oppose them.

In this tactic the Chinese were initially successful and the Tibetan soldiers disappeared from their path into the mountains. For a time it seemed as if 'peaceful liberation' would indeed work. No one, least of all the Chinese, realized that the unopposed frontier crossing was only a deceptively quiet overture to a campaign which would last for a decade and reach its climax in a national uprising.

When news of the Chinese incursion spread beyond the Himalayas it was regarded by the 'free world' as simply another example of militant Communism on the march. By 1950 the cold war had thoroughly invested Europe while in the Far East troops

43

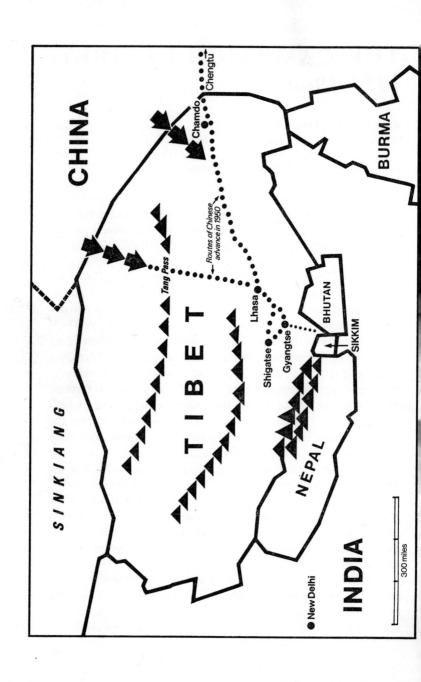

of the United Nations were fighting desperate battles with the North Koreans; in Indo-China the French were heavily engaged with the Viet Minh, and in Malaya the British Army was struggling to contain the onslaught of Red terrorists from the jungles. The East appeared to be 'going Red' with a vengeance, and America and those European countries with empires to defend against the flood-tide of Communism and nationalism had enough to do without worrying too much about a Chinese foray into a remote land of forbidding, snow-capped heights and open plateaux of vast extent. Tibet, which had long before turned its back on the rest of the world, found itself without a friend. China's explanation for her action was accepted with hardly a demur.

And it had to be admitted that her case was a good one. It rested on the simple premise that Tibet belonged to China, that it had always been an integral part of the Middle Kingdom, and that the PLA was freeing its people from medieval bondage. The historical record shows that there is a sound basis for the Chinese claim to suzerainty and some authorities go so far as to declare it unchallengeable in international law. During the Manchu Dynasty in the early 18th century Peking established firm control over Tibet, but its grip was loosened as the Celestial Empire went into decline, and later governments were unable to enforce their authority over the region. Tibet's case for independence was and still is argued on the ground that her Han conquerors were driven out in 1911 and freedom was established in that year.

Much of the confusion over Tibet's status stems from a conference at Simla in 1913 when China, Tibet and British India made an attempt to iron out an agreement on its frontiers. The results of these deliberations was the division of the country into two zones, Outer Tibet and Inner Tibet, the latter being nearer to China and including a region known as Eastern Tibet. Peking's suzerainty over the whole of Tibet was recognized at the conference. Shortly after signing the draft agreement, however, China raised an objection to the 'Inner and Outer' classification. The document was never ratified, but the crucial fact was that China did not abdicate her acknowledged suzerainty and continued to rule Eastern Tibet as part of the province of Sikang. It is worth noting that, as regards Tibet, the Nationalist Government in Taiwan takes the same stand as its supplanters in Peking, and all official maps show the country as part of the Chinese mainland.

After the Simla talks Tibet retired from the 20th century. Once again it became the Hidden Land, a Shangri-la where nomads lived high among the clouds, where monks spun prayer wheels at their Buddhist devotions, where all paid homage to a God-King, the Dalai Lama, and some exported yak tails for use as Santa Claus beards. The First and Second World Wars came and went, leaving Tibet untouched and the majority of its people unaware that they had ever been fought.

This isolation was made possible by geography but was re-inforced by a deliberate policy of restricting contacts with the outside world to a bare minimum. In this way, so the leaders in Tibet reasoned, the people, the majority of whom were believed to be gentled by their age-old religion, could continue to live in peace alongside potentially aggressive neighbours. It was a policy founded on self-deception. Reality caught up with Tibet in the autumn of 1950 when Peking radio announced to the world that the 'peaceful liberation' of the Tibetan peoples was under way.

Frequent warnings of China's intention towards Tibet were given by Communist leaders towards the end of 1949, but the decision to embark on the expedition was not taken until the following spring, probably after the return of Chairman Mao Tse-tung from a prolonged visit to Moscow during which time he signed a defensive pact with Russia and received a promise of military assistance. It was intended that the take-over operation should be completed by late summer.

Why Mao decided on this particular moment for the invasion has never been revealed but with the hindsight of history some deductions may now be made.

First of all, let us take a look at the situation in China in the early days of 1950. For the first time in twenty years the country was at peace, affording the new regime an opportunity to tackle its main tasks – the consolidation of power and authority and the reconstruction of a war-ruined economy. The problems were immense and in dealing with them the PLA had a major part to play. There was the important matter of securing and occupying the whole country. Various pockets of Nationalist resistance in some of the remote provinces and regions remained to be mopped up. On Mao's own admission there were then at large 400,000 Kuomintang guerrillas, while on the island of Taiwan the defeated Chiang Kai-shek was building a fortress refuge.

Taiwan was already a thorn in the Communist flesh and the Third Field Army had been given the job of removing it in the summer, once the Army's training in amphibious warfare had been completed. Mao may have savoured the prospect of announcing simultaneously the liberation of Tibet and the fall of Taiwan, less than a year after the founding of the People's Republic. As it turned out, this pleasure was denied him.

But there were other concerns of a military and domestic nature. The size of the PLA itself was already a headache for a regime well aware of the dangers posed by large standing armies. During the civil war the various Field Armies had swelled their ranks to an estimated four-and-a-half million men in the year of final victory. So many men under arms presented not only a potential threat of counter-revolution; they also formed a drain on public finances at a time when the menace of inflation was growing. The Army had to be reduced in order to release men for more productive work. This was partly solved by the semi-demobilizing of thousands of soldiers, putting them to work on the land and weeding out many of the former Nationalists who had 'gone over' during 1949.

In the midst of this confused situation at home, aggravated by the introduction of various agrarian reforms which clearly required decisions as to their order of importance, the command was issued to take Tibet. From what followed it is obvious that little planning or forethought had gone into the military side of the operation.

The explanation for this and the sudden, almost impulsive way in which the expedition was ordered can be traced to the character of the Chairman. Although well-known for his outward phlegm, on public occasions at least, in the days immediately following the civil war Mao was vigorous in decision, anxious for quick results, with his patience, like that of most of his fellow Hunanese, burning on a short fuse. Military success had also bred over-confidence, illustrated in October 1949 by a rash and ill-prepared seaborne lunge at the Nationalist-held off-shore island of Quemoy which had resulted in the death through battle or drowning of 13,000 men and the further loss of 7000 prisoners.

Mao's motives for the Tibetan adventure stemmed from a number of considerations, some of them strategic. After the Simla Agreement, Tibet had fallen within the British sphere of influence and remained so until India gained its independence. Mao was anxious to fill this political vacuum with soldiers and secure the country and its distant frontier against Indian influence. Occupation would also seal off the area from any Nationalist remnants who might be tempted to hole up there. It may also have crossed his agile mind that, with Tibet once secured, another route could be opened into Sinkiang Province which for more than a century had hung on the brink of becoming a Russian appendage.

But the biggest single factor which prompted the order to invade in the face of more immediate domestic problems was national pride.

As we saw earlier, China has a gnawing ache, an all-consuming desire to win back either through negotiation or if necessary limited war what has been taken from her in the past, in the days of the unequal treaties. For more than a hundred years, since the days when the dragon was first awakened, then humiliated and its fire extinguished, the goal that China has set herself is the retrieving of her self-respect – and this is not be confused with 'face'. The Communist regime has a keen awareness of the hurt inflicted by predators from the West, and lasting memories of the hated international settlements, compounds and concessions with their 'Europeans only' rules. In its sense of pride in race and culture, its upholding of the thousand and one precedents laid down during the twenty-one dynasties especially in regard to territory and frontiers, the Government's attitude is no different from that of previous Emperors, the former holders of the 'mandate of heaven'.

It is this combination of national pride, revolutionary zeal and strategic objectives which set the soldiers on the march to Tibet. Tibet came first because she seemed easy for the taking, unlikely to resist for very long, if at all, and because no other country was in a position to help her even if it had wanted to do so. But within a year of the order going out Peking must have regretted its haste, for by that time China was in direct confrontation with America on the battlefields of Korea, and Tibet was resisting occupation on a scale never contemplated. Chinese soldiers were campaigning on two fronts, with all that entails, and the invasion of Taiwan, so dear to Mao's heart, had been postponed indefinitely.

The troops detailed for the Tibetan expedition were from the 1st and 2nd Field Armies, seven divisions totalling about 35,000 men. Five were allotted from the 2nd Army which at the end of the civil war found itself in occupation of much of southern China and is believed to have provided assistance to Ho Chi Minh and the Viet Minh who were operating from bases just across the Yunnan frontier.

Peng Teh-huai, commander of the 1st Field Army and a future Minister of Defence, must have felt the loss of two divisions for the other component of the force, since he was engaged in the strenuous task of pushing Communist control into some of the more inaccessible regions of the north-west, including Sinkiang.

That so small a force was provided for the 'liberation' demonstrates both Peking's unawareness of the immensity of the task they had given both commanders and men, and of the difficulty in gathering an army for what was an extraneous task when considered alongside the whole range of duties the PLA was expected to perform at that time. If Mao had waited no more than three years, he could have accomplished his aim quickly and effectively with a readily available, properly equipped force of a size sufficient for the job. The spark of Tibetan resistance could then have been snuffed out without giving it the opportunity of igniting the flame of national revolt.

As it was, the generals decided on a two-pronged thrust with the five-division force moving westwards through Szechwan and

The Chinese Red Army

Sikang* and the two divisions striking down into Tibet from Tsinghai Province. The two arms of the force began their approach marches behind schedule and soon ran into difficulties. Not only had they to secure the outlying provinces from the Nationalists as they moved along but the terrain in the extreme western regions of China is hard going at the best of times. In 1950 roads and bridges were either primitive or non-existent. The proposed timetable for advance and occupation quickly became a work of fiction. For much of the route to the frontier zone the troops had to lay aside their arms and get down to building roads over, round and across mountain ranges. Rivers, ravines and gorges had more often than not to be bridged to enable lorry transport to bring up supplies and provisions. The Red Army was used to living off the country, but the two lines of march led across an area which could offer very little. Mountainous, wild and inhospitable, it was similar to what the troops were about to face in Tibet.

The construction work carried out during the summer months was a considerable feat of engineering. During the civil war the Communist forces had of necessity developed a talent for overcoming physical obstacles. They had become masters of adaptation with a flair for ingenious, if temporary, solutions to seemingly insurmountable problems. Battalions could switch from the role of infantry to that of coolie gangs at the drop of a shovel or pick – equipment ranking in order of importance next to the rifle and the bayonet.

By October, when the leaves on the sparse trees were falling and a fresh bite could be felt in the winds whipping round the mountains and through the passes, the forward infantry elements reached Tibet. Peking had by now opened its propaganda campaign and agents had been infiltrated ahead of the army to start a 'fifth column' movement. Uncertainty and jitters afflicted both Tibetan Government and people. It has been suggested that the propaganda war was launched because of China's doubt over the validity of its claim to suzerainty; that by repeated assertions it hoped to convince itself and others of the justice of its action. This was not so. China was not troubled by self-doubt, but the

* Abolished on 18 June 1955, and divided up between Tibet and Szechwan.

political leaders in Peking and the generals on the spot were concerned that there should be as little fighting as possible – and for good reason. The less resistance there was, the more the occupation could be represented as being welcomed by the down-trodden Tibetans. But the worries of the generals were more urgent. Winter was approaching and if the Tibetans chose to fight then there was a real danger of the Chinese divisions, already tired from months of construction work, getting tied down and perhaps hopelessly trapped among mountain passes deep in snow and ice. Moreover, the likelihood of Chinese troops becoming embroiled in the Korean War was growing daily. If that happened, then Korea would head the list of demands for men and supplies, and the occupation force would be left to fend for itself, with the terrible prospect, at least in Chinese eyes, of a humiliating setback. A peaceful invasion was more than ever the object of the exercise.

The first test of the effectiveness of the propaganda and 'noise war' came soon after the advanced units crossed into Tibet proper on 7 October.

Chamdo, a town and outpost situated on the main route from China, offered a natural defensive position. The Tibetan Army had reinforced it soon after news of Chinese intentions had reached the capital city, Lhasa. The garrison now consisted of about 3000 ill-equipped, nervous soldiers whose heaviest weapons were a few ancient 12-pdrs. This motley gathering was expected to hurl back the invaders. Having scouted the position on the evening of the 13th, the Chinese bivouacked, started big camp fires and rent the night with bugle calls and slogan shouting. By first light the Tibetans had vanished. Chamdo, the gateway to half a million square miles of Central Asia, fell without a shot fired. The 700-mile road to Lhasa, their principal objective, lay open.

Seizing the opportunity, the Chinese followed up quickly and within a week had rounded up or killed at least half of the officers and men of the scattered force. They captured the governor of the Chamdo area, Ngabon Ngawang Jigme, a member of the Tibetan Kashag or Cabinet, who quickly turned pro-Chinese and was to prove a pliant and valuable tool in the future administration.

The Chinese Red Army

This initial success must have heartened and encouraged the Chinese, but their objective was not to be achieved as easily as the first weeks of October suggested. There were others who were not prepared to follow the Tibetan Army's example of putting discretion before valour. Eastern Tibet, through which the PLA was moving, was the homeland of the Khambas, a wild mountain tribe, used to acting upon their own initiative and taking orders from Lhasa only when the mood suited them. These nomadic warriors knew no boundaries or frontiers. They pitched their camps in Tibet, the Eastern Region, Sikang, and as far east as Szechwan. They eked out a precarious living from the uncertain produce of the sheltered mountainsides, from their herds of goats and cattle, and more enjoyably by raiding caravans, exacting tolls on travellers and imposing their own form of import duties on the passage and trade of tea and ponies. Those of the tribe who inhabited the plateaux did rather better and made some profits out of wool exports.

In Sikang the Chinese authorities had learned to leave them well alone, and merchants had long accepted that to pay dues to the Khambas was the only way to stay in business.

Supported by neighbouring tribes, the Amdos and the Goloks, who were aligned with the Khambas in their hatred of the Chinese, the tribesmen went to war, replacing the Army. And they fought in the way of all nomadic, mountain peoples. As the Red soldiers probed and moved cautiously along the passes and narrow defiles, they were harassed and ambushed. It was reported at the time that a whole division was trapped in the mountains and annihilated after having been detached from the main line of advance to deal with a rumoured gathering of Tibetan Army units. This report has never been substantiated, although Khamba refugees swear to the truth of it. What is beyond doubt is that the nomad warriors cut off large numbers of Chinese and slaughtered them. The Khambas took no prisoners and against their traditional foes they practised revolting cruelties. Fighting in bands of rarely more than a hundred, they must have presented a terrifying sight to isolated Chinese detachments as they charged down boulder-strewn mountainsides on sure-footed ponies, firing rifles from the hip and swinging their swords. Many Chinese died under the hooves of their frenzied ponies while many others, unfortunate enough to be captured, were mutilated before being thrown over a precipice or into a river.

These Cossacks of the slopes wore knee-length, shaggy boots with tight riding-breeches and woollen tunics, in the folds of which they tucked food and ammunition. Their horsemanship was superb and, unusually for mountain warriors, they preferred hand-to-hand combat with sword and knife to long-distance sniping. The infantryman with rifle and bayonet was no match for these lovers of in-fighting.

The Khambas avoided large concentrations of Red Troops; they swooped on small units left behind to guard the route of advance, they cut off supply trucks inching their way along primitive roads, they murdered pickets thrown too far forward and harassed work gangs repairing the main highway. Their favourite tactics were either to ambush units by rolling boulders down the mountains to block narrow defiles or to pour boiling water from some lofty crag on unsuspecting soldiers below. This barbaric and medieval warfare not unnaturally infuriated the Chinese who began to respond in kind. The Khambas had not the men, the means or the skill to engage the invaders in pitched battles. They could only raid and disrupt. But the Chinese had no taste for this guerrilla conflict, though some ten years earlier they had themselves become masters of it against the Japanese. The advance was reduced to a crawl and with the onset of winter it stalled.

These were worrying days for the 'liberators'. For lack of previous planning many regiments were without winter clothing and the casualty toll through cold and frost-bite was about 2000. Fever also seems to have swept some units at this stage of the campaign and to have claimed another 3000 men. Because of the frequent ambushes and the poor state of the roads all the way back to Szechwan convoys were infrequent and unreliable. The Chinese suffered from shortage of food, ammunition and medical supplies. Casualties could not be replaced, since the armies then fighting in Korea were being given top priority.

The Chinese Red Army

But even if the Tibetans had realized the full extent of the Chinese troubles there was little they could do other than maraud. Furthermore the practice of taking no prisoners rebounded on the Khambas since they had no one to train them in the use of the heavier infantry weapons they captured. So machine-guns and mortars were useless to them, and went the same way as their pitiable captives. If this equipment could have been brought into use it would have considerably aided and sustained Tibetan resistance and taken a heavier toll than the estimated 10,000 casualties suffered by the Chinese between October 1950 and the following spring.

Meanwhile the Tibetan Government had been active on the political front. The Dalai Lama, not quite sixteen at the time of the invasion and therefore below the required age, was nevertheless on 17 November invested with full sovereign powers. On 18 December he moved with his advisers and the senior members of his Government to Yatung, a town near the Indian border. The Indian Government was requested to raise the matter of Chinese aggression at the United Nations on Tibet's behalf, but Mr Nehru refused. In reply he suggested that Tibet should raise the matter herself directly.

Tibet attempted to do so by circulating an 'unofficial note' to the members of the Security Council. Four delegations were prepared to visit Britain, America, India and Nepal, with the object of seeking support for a direct appeal at the U.N. but Tibet's efforts to gain recognition and help for her plight met with nothing but discouragement. The price was being paid for centuries of deliberate seclusion. No one wanted to know. Tibet was politically and militarily isolated. With the coming of spring, when the snows began to melt in the passes and defiles and the spearheads of the two Chinese armies once more started to thrust forward, Tibet faced and accepted the inevitable.

In April Chairman Mao invited a Tibetan delegation to Peking to discuss future political arrangements. Included in the group was the former governor of the Chamdo area, Ngabon Ngawang Jigme, and the Panchen Lama, who ranked second only in status and importance to the Dalai Lama. On 23 May a settlement, sometimes known as the 17-point Agreement, was signed. The 'liberation' was thus formalized and legalized, but the Chinese had to wait until October before the Dalai Lama intimated his acceptance of the Agreement.

The Panchen Lama, himself also a teenager, returned home and thereafter acted as a Communist puppet. In subsequently playing the Panchen Lama off against the Dalai Lama the Chinese were following the traditional practice of the Manchu Emperors in their dealings with the rulers of Tibet.

On 8 August 1951, the first official representative of the Peking regime arrived in Lhasa. General Chang Ching-wu immediately began talks with senior members of the Government on ways of carrying out the Agreement, which allowed for a Tibetan regional administration to have charge of domestic affairs but to have no say in foreign policy. Two days after accepting the Agreement, the Dalai Lama on 26 October watched the five divisions of Lieut.-General Chang Kuo-hua parade through Lhasa. On 1 December the other two divisions which had approached from the north-west also reached the outskirts of the capital. Tibet was once again in Chinese hands and the two Changs were to guide the country's affairs for the next fifteen years. The wheel had come full circle.

The Army of occupation, considerably reinforced after the losses of the winter, now found itself in charge of a population variously estimated at between one and two million. Since Tibet knew nothing of any census, and so many of its peoples were nomadic, population figures up to the arrival of the Chinese can only be loosely estimated. At this time a further two million Tibetans or people recognizing the spiritual authority of the Dalai Lama inhabited the neighbouring Chinese provinces of Sinkiang and Sikang, and the countries of Sikkim, Bhutan and Nepal. The terrain over which the Army had to spread itself averages around 11,000 feet above sea-level, its mountainous regions alternating with fertile plains and valleys; in the north is the desolate and bitterly cold plain known as Chang Tang, the home of many nomadic tribes. Both in geography and climate the country has sometimes been likened to Switzerland.

The Chinese Red Army

In the first year of the take-over the Army's grip on the country was not oppressive. This was a period, indeed the only period, when soldiers and officials made sincere efforts to win the support, goodwill and co-operation of the people. The Army and 'work personnel' concentrated on opening up the country, developing communications back to China by road and air. Two major arteries, one through the then still existing Province of Sikang to the Szechwan railhead at Chengtu and the other out from Tibet and through Tsinghai Province, were constructed out of the existing rough tracks. Once again the soldiers showed considerable engineering skills. The Tibet–Sikang highway is believed to be the highest road in the world with an average height of 13,000 feet above sea-level, crossing fourteen mountain ranges and twelve rivers; the Tsinghai highway traverses mountains, swampland and the stark northern plain.

Both roads were completed in 1954 and have since been pushed beyond Lhasa to towns near the Indian frontier. Tibetan labour was used in the construction of some stretches. The majority of the local workers, though described as volunteers, were press-ganged, and the Government was forced to contribute large sums towards the costs.

While pushing ahead with the programme to open up the country, the Chinese set about abolishing the enslavement of the serfs by land and tax reform, and new methods of cultivation and food storage (thus downgrading the status and importance of the monasteries), but progress was slow. The peasants, supposed beneficiaries of the changes, passively resisted what they regarded as a deliberate attempt to destroy their way of life while aristocrats and monks, their feudal overlords, conspired to retain their ancient rights and privileges. But Chinese patience soon wore thin, and coercion came to be used increasingly. Strong-arm methods, employed against a people with a pronounced streak of stubbornness, achieved only the reverse of what was intended, and the number of incidents of protest and local revolt began to mount. Full of revolutionary earnestness, dismayed at blank-faced intransigence and under pressure from Peking, the Chinese administrators, who were fronted by Tibetan collaborators and those trying to make the best out of a difficult situation, over-reacted and became progressively more ruthless. The number of executions, public beatings and cases of torture rose; thousands were sent to labour camps and youngsters from the better-off families were dispatched to Peking for political indoctrination.

This situation, which meant that the Chinese advanced their reforms by three strides, only to take two back later, lasted until 1956 when a major uprising rocked the country. It began, not surprisingly, among the nomadic tribes of Eastern Tibet whose capacity for resistance had been consistently underestimated. The Khambas, Amdos and Goloks were alarmed at the way in which they were losing their lands to settlers from China. These imported 'colonists' were said, to number millions, though at this stage thousands would be a likelier estimate. Sent in as part of a deliberate policy to increase Tibet's population and eventually to dominate it with Chinese, the newcomers not only robbed the tribes of their traditional lands but upset the delicately balanced food situation by their introduction of new methods of farming, storage and distribution. After a number of poor harvests it was the Tibetans who suffered because most of the monasteries were no longer able to help; what food there was went in the first instance to Chinese. Seeing their lands taken over, feeling their stomachs empty, with no more caravans to raid, no merchants upon whom to levy tolls, with the wool trade almost at a standstill, and their religion threatened, the tribes rose up. They took to their ponies and resorted to war.

Once again lonely outposts, supply trucks, work gangs, small detachments of troops on the march were ambushed and attacked. The settlers were murdered by the score. As a sign of defiance one tribe returned a group of prisoners, all with their noses sliced off.

The tribesmen had learned some lessons from their earlier battles in 1950 and this time they formed a unified command of chieftains who had overall direction of the struggle to rid their lands of the hated Chinese. The gathered warrriors called themselves Tensoong Magar (Regiments of the Guardians of Religion) and included boys and women in their ranks. The chiefs may have entertained the idea of meeting the Chinese in pitched battle and, instead of killing all their prisoners, attempting to get from them instruction on the weapons they had captured.

But the PLA declined the invitation to battle and called in the air force as a cheaper and more effective way of dispersing the rebels. Concentrations of tribesmen were bombed and a number of monasteries shelled. Chinese generals have always had a liking for artillery and they put it to good use in Tibet. The warriors, unable to comprehend this form of warfare and somewhat demoralized by air attacks, broke up into smaller bands and proved elusive when bombardments and air strikes were cautiously followed up by the Army. Usually the tribesmen were given too much time and opportunity to disappear, and although the Army was able to restore its authority over large tracts of rebel territory, it was unable to come to grips with the rebels and defeat them in the field.

The size and scale of the trouble rattled the Chinese administrators in Lhasa and, acting on their advice, Peking called a halt to the reform programme. This move had little or no effect on the tribesmen who continued their hit-and-run tactics through 1957 and into the following year. But Chinese pressure began to tell and in late 1958 the chiefs decided to fall back on Central Tibet in the hope of replenishing their supplies of food and ammunition. An estimated 20,000 made this exodus by one route or another. As they drew nearer to Lhasa local sympathizers gave them access to secret stores. This infused fresh life into the rebel cause, and thousands of new recruits began to flock to their standards. By March 1959, the uprising had become almost nation-wide.

There was a little more to it, however, than just the success of the Khambas infecting other Tibetans. The roots of the expanding crisis were to be found beyond Tibet in neighbouring Sinkiang and Tsinghai, both of which had substantial populations of religious minorities, Muslims as well as Lamaists. In these provinces the Communists had forcibly extended their programme of introducing rural communes, to which there was considerable local resistance. The Tibetan minority's recognition of the authority of the Dalai Lama and their steadfast resistance to revolutionary socialism convinced Peking that it had been a mistake to call a halt to reform in Tibet while pushing ahead with it in adjoining regions. The two approaches were not compatible, according to Mao and his lieutenants. So Party cadres were summoned from Tibet to China to study how the communes worked, and the Dalai Lama was invited to Peking for talks. Realizing that the truce on reform was at an end and that the Dalai Lama might be in some danger if he left Lhasa, the whole of Tibet grew restless and eventually joined in the struggle upon which the Khambas and others had already embarked. Though Tibetan autonomy had always been a piece of political make-believe, it was now viewed in Peking as an obstacle to the development of Communist programmes and ideals – not merely in Tibet but in the other western provinces. The revolt of the tribes hardened Chinese attitudes and decided Peking on an all-out campaign directed at suppressing the rebels and completely absorbing Tibet within the mainland.

This new policy of toughness could hardly be expected to do anything but unite the Tibetans, particularly when the position of the Dalai Lama was clearly threatened; but the Communists were tired of temporizing and had decided to bring matters to a conclusion.

In the early days of March the struggle grew in bitterness and intensity, and on the 17th fighting broke out in Lhasa. The Dalai Lama saw as his first duty the ensuring of the survival of Lamaism and acting on the wish of his advisers, he fled the capital. A sandstorm and the garb of a peasant facilitated his escape into the country where he eventually met up with a party of Khambas. He had toyed with the idea of setting up a government in rebel-controlled territory but on learning of some vicious acts of Chinese retaliation he travelled on to find sanctuary in India.

Meanwhile the Khambas, who at one time had contemplated moving on Lhasa in force, heard that the Chinese were freely using artillery and mortars on monasteries and public buildings in the capital. They broke up into two main parties. Some 10,000 of them moved south-east to the Lhoka region and *en route* captured fourteen Army outposts and small garrisons. For a short period they re-established Tibetan rule in the region. The other and larger force made its way back to Kham Province to continue the fight on familiar territory.

Rebel bands were now forming throughout the country, their total numbers being estimated at around 50,000. Taking advantage of temporary Chinese confusion, some groups acted boldly. At Gongbo, for instance, a town on the Lhasa–Chamdo road, 700 Tibetans were reported to have stormed in and overwhelmed the garrison while south of Lhasa at Tsedang the Chinese were said to have suffered a thousand casualties, including a general killed.

Now, for the first time since China had occupied Tibet a decade earlier, the world sat up and took notice. The flight of the Dalai Lama, stories of heroic and fierce resistance against 'hordes' of Chinese, helped to fire the imagination of the world. The Himalayan hill stations of India were flooded with journalists seeking stories from among the 85,000 refugees to feed the appetites of their readers hungry for news of a strange war on the roof of the world. But very few people had much idea of what was really taking place in Tibet and much of the reporting was a combination of imagination and wishful thinking. There was a war on, certainly, but it was one which had to be reported from the impenetrable sidelines.

Many of the stories were diverting, if nothing else. The Chinese, for example, were reported to be setting off atomic explosions in order to melt the Himalayan snows, presumably with the object of drowning the rebels! Chinese soldiers were said to be attacking their officers, for no very clear reason. The casualty figures given, if added together over a three-month period, would have denuded the country of half its population and left but a remnant of the PLA's original strength.

The stories coming out of Tibet, both the accurate and the improbable, inflamed world opinion against China. Malaya, which was newly independent and suspicious of Chinese intentions in South-East Asia, in conjunction with Eire raised Tibet's plight at the United Nations. Strong denunciations of Chinese actions also came from India, which was feeling increasingly uncomfortable about its borders with China. But apart from these verbal attacks on 'expansionist' China, nothing was done to aid Tibet – for the simple reason that nothing could be.

The Chinese had enough on their hands without bothering about the deprecations of an impotent U.N. They had got themselves into a difficult situation and in spite of considerable reinforcements the PLA was having a great deal of trouble regaining the initiative.

By the late spring of 1959 the rebels had established themselves in three main areas: to the north in Kham and Amdo territory, in the mountains south of Lhasa and to the south-west of the capital in a region bordering the Indian frontier.

General Chang Kuo-hua, who had the task of directing the campaign of suppression, once again called on aircraft to bomb gatherings of tribesmen and mountain redoubts. He also launched a food-denial campaign and by ordering his commanders to be circumspect in attack he denied the tribesmen the opportunity both of engaging their enemy and of capturing much needed weapons and supplies. General Chang concentrated first on the rebel groups to the south of Lhasa and eventually succeeded in closing the Himalayan passes. It was suspected in Lhasa that Western agents had played a share in instigating the revolt and that attempts were being made to get supplies to the rebels through the passes. These suspicions may not have been totally unjustified and from time to time unidentified aircraft were reported over Tibet. These mysterious aircraft may have been on supply missions since refugees were later able to describe parachutes and parachute silk, of which they could have had no previous knowledge.

But even if limited amounts of arms and ammunition did get through, they made no difference to the outcome of the fighting. With the passes sealed, and the escape routes of refugees closed, the PLA had the rebels south of Lhasa boxed in. Throughout the summer the tribesmen were bombed and harried from the air, and shelled from long distance. They were squeezed relentlessly until in desperation the regiments broke up and tried to break out. Many groups were caught and wiped out, others managed to slip through and make their way north to Kham and Amdo areas. By the autumn the rebellion was over. Some 250,000 troops were deployed throughout the country while the surviving rebels, about 20,000, dispersed among the more inaccessible regions, no longer constituted a threat. Once the Chinese had recovered their nerve and co-ordinated their strategy, the Tibetans did not stand a chance. In view of the size of the Chinese Army in Tibet it is amazing that the Tibetan rebels were able to sustain their campaign for nearly four years. This was due to a number of reasons. The Chinese forces often acted in a dilatory manner but this was because of Peking's mixed and changing political objectives. The Army was never quite sure which it was meant to be doing, fighting rebels or reforming them. Once Peking had decided on war as an extension of its Tibetan policy the Army acted swiftly and with determination.

Military success was followed by a complete take-over of all Tibetan institutions; in an attempt to destroy for ever the influence of Lamaism the monasteries were destroyed, monks were sent in their thousands to labour camps, hundreds were killed. The whole fabric of Tibetan life was ripped apart and it is doubtful if it will ever be put together again.

There have been occasional rumbles of unrest among the nomads since 1959 but they are no longer in a position to embarrass the Chinese.

The exiled Dalai Lama summed up the picture in 1966 when he said: 'The Chinese are being settled in Tibet on such a massive scale that soon there will be no Tibet. Monasteries and all traces of Tibetan religion and culture are being destroyed and the Communists have turned the country into an armed camp.' And sadly he added: 'I do not think that armed rebellion by my people against the Chinese can succeed at this stage. So sending arms will only encourage false hopes.'

A year after these words were spoken the Tibetans were given a chance to cause some disruption. The Cultural Revolution had spread to Tibet and in February fighting broke out between Red Guards and regular units of the Army. General Chang sent in a battalion of the 155th Regiment, which stormed Red Guards strongpoints and quickly restored Army authority. There were other incidents up and down the country; all were put down by the Army. If the Tibetans had been able to exploit this opportunity created by internal dissension then no doubt they would have done so. But nothing happened. The Tibetans stood by and watched the Chinese fight and squabble among themselves. The will to resist had been completely broken.

For the Tibetans the debit side of the liberation account is full of harrowing entries, including the estimated 90,000 people reported by the International Commission of Jurists to have been killed in battle or executed between the years 1950 and 1959. But there is a credit side. Schools, hospitals, health centres and a few factories have been built and jobs have followed the military with the massive construction programme for roads, garrisons and airfields.

China's absorption of the country carried a high initial cost in terms of its men and resources, but in Peking's eyes this was small beer compared to the gains it brought. The settlers, whose removal from China eased problems of population and land shortage in their home localities, are making Tibet into a more productive country, while improved communications have enabled China to obtain a firmer control over the once troublesome provinces bordering Tibet and Russia. In the Himalayas she has a secure frontier against India.

The success with which China has digested the great lump of Central Asia can perhaps best be judged by the fact that in 1965 Tibet was once again designated an autonomous region and in 1970 it was downgraded from a Military Region to a District – sure signs of Peking's confidence in the process of assimilation.

And General Chang Kuo-hua, who spent seventeen years of his life trying to impose the dictates of Chinese Communism on a recalcitrant population, escaped Mao's displeasure at his treatment of the Red Guards, and perhaps in recognition of his Tibetan services was appointed commissar of the Chengtu Military Region in Szechwan. For General Chang too the wheel of life came full circle, for it was from Chengtu that he set out in the autumn of 1950 to liberate peacefully the Land of the Lamas. The general died in Chengtu in February 1972, and was buried with full military honours. A memorial service was held for him in Lhasa.

THE KOREAN WAR: 1950-1953

The laws of war in each historical stage
have their characteristics and cannot be
mechanically applied in a different age –
Mao Tse-tung

The dash to the Yalu River was in full swing. The North Korean
Army was in desperate and disorganized retreat and it seemed to
the majority of those serving in the United Nations forces in
October 1950 that the war which had engulfed the Korean peninsula for five savage months would be over by Christmas at the
latest. To be sure, China was making threatening noises, but the
United Nations' High Command, particularly the Commander-
in-Chief, General Douglas MacArthur, dismissed these as
bellicose diplomatic posturings and endeavoured to keep up the
momentum of the advance northward. And just as little regard
was paid to what the intelligence reports from the fluid front were
indicating: that the Chinese were not just talking about intervening
in the war, they were in it already.

In the headlong rush to the Yalu and the Chinese border the
7th Regiment of the 6th Division of the South Korean Army got
itself well out in front. Early in October forward elements of the
regiment scouted the river and the desolate, uninviting country
through which it flowed; not even the warm, autumnal tints for
which Korea, 'the land of morning calm', is noted could soften the
brooding atmosphere of this seemingly deserted frontier land.
The 7th, satisfied with its reconnaissance, turned back down the
route of approach – and disappeared. Days were to pass before
the regiment was heard of again. It transpired that the 7th had
unwittingly strayed into a staging area for the Chinese armies
gathering in secret across the Yalu. In an effort to conceal their
presence on Korean soil the Chinese had attempted to annihilate
the trespassing regiment. They need not have been so ruthless.

E

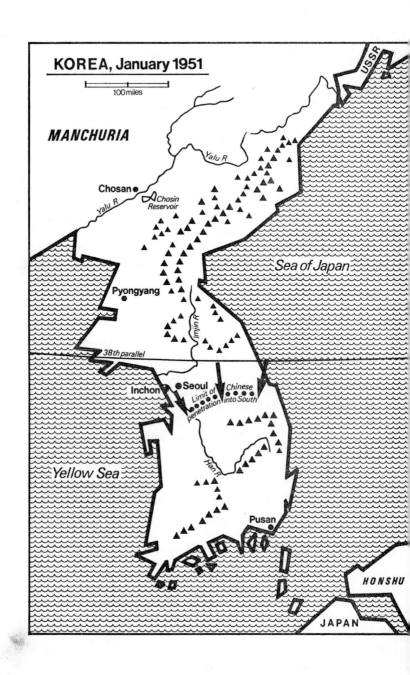

KOREA, January 1951

100 miles

MANCHURIA

USSR

Yalu R

Chosan

Chosin Reservoir

Yalu R

Sea of Japan

Pyongyang

Imjin R

38th parallel

Inchon

Seoul

Limit of penetration

Chinese into South

Yellow Sea

Han R

Pusan

HONSHU

JAPAN

The reports of the handful of survivors who reached the U.N. lines were either ignored or given little credence.

Meanwhile, on 26 October in another sector South Korean troops clashed with Chinese soldiers near the Chosin Reservoir and took a number of prisoners who were later identified as coming from the 124th Division of the PLA. A few days later in the same area, United States Marines knocked out some prowling Chinese tanks and also took prisoners. These were men from the 126th Division. Both the 124th and 126th were known to form part of the Chinese 42nd Army. And at about this time rumours began to percolate through to the U.N. commanders that units of the 39th and 40th Armies were crossing the Yalu.

Incredible as it may seem, the High Command remained unmoved by the increasing amount of evidence that the Chinese were deploying in strength. This refusal to accept what was clearly happening – regimental commanders, it must be said, were more apprehensive than their seniors – had a great deal to do with MacArthur. The victor of the Pacific War and the man who had pulled off the daring master-stroke of the Inchon landings thought the threat of Chinese intervention was greatly exaggerated. MacArthur's prestige and reputation had never stood higher, his subordinates went in awe of him, and, as an American said later, if the General had announced that he was going to walk on water, few in the autumn of 1950 would have doubted his ability to do so.

MacArthur's perverse attitude naturally communicated itself down the chain of command, while in the field U.N. soldiers, who for weeks had seen nothing but the backs of North Koreans in retreat, could scent the end of the war, demobilization or more pleasant postings, and they also did not want to believe the evidence of their own patrolling and occasional clashes, that the Chinese were around somewhere and probably in strength.

Another factor which aided the Chinese build-up in Korea was the manner in which the U.N. forces advanced. There was no effective overall control of the movement to the border, units lost touch with each other as the nature of the country made communications extremely difficult; no regimental or brigade commander could be sure of what was happening on his flanks, over the hills and mountains to his left and right. It was a badly planned, ineptly handled advance, to establish contact with no one seemed to know quite what, in the general direction of the Chinese border. It was a military mess, one which invited disaster and for which MacArthur was solely responsible.

That being said, the Commander-in-Chief's appalling blunders cannot detract from the Red Army's brilliant feat of moving some 250,000 men from Manchuria into North Korea and completely deceiving the U.N. Command as to their numbers and positions. It was the type of operation in which the PLA had a lot of experience, but this was probably the biggest in its experience and it was carried out under the direction of Lin Piao with consummate skill. The Red soldiers slipped across the Yalu either by bridge or boat under cover of darkness, and thereafter hid by day and moved to their concentration points by night. Even then they usually avoided roads and crossed country which could hide their tracks. They hid in caves, disused mines, woods and camouflaged mountain retreats. Some disguised themselves as Koreans and lived in villages and on farms. It was small wonder that U.N. air reconnaissance failed to detect any signs of large bodies of troops, except for known North Korean units attempting to re-group.

This secret manoeuvring into position was a preparatory move by the Chinese political and military leaders in a war plan which had alternative endings. If the U.N. forces pressed on toward the Chinese border in defiance of warnings to stay back, then the armies for the counter-thrust would be ready to strike from their hidden bases; but should the U.N. hesitate, then a show of force might bring a decision for MacArthur's armies to fall back to the 38th Parallel and a wider war could then be avoided. In retrospect it now seems that some of the engagements between Chinese and American or South Korean troops were deliberately brought on in late October as a sort of mailed-fist threat. But General MacArthur, with the concurrence of President Truman and the acquiescence of the U.N., was determined to overrun the whole of North Korea and place troops along the Manchurian border. He was not prepared to listen to those who were advising caution.

He pressed on towards the Yalu and the first war in history between China and America became inevitable; and his generalship was such that the United Nations forces were in no position to repel the Chinese assault when it came.*

MacArthur's arrogance drove him to the débâcle in North Korea, but the politicians in Washington and the United Nations also bear a heavy responsibility for allowing a local war to develop into a major conflict. They could not resist the temptation of uniting Korea by force of arms, and badly miscalculated China's determination and ability to prevent this.

To place China in the context of Korea it is necessary to look back briefly at the years immediately after the Japanese surrender in 1945. Troops of the United States and Russia went into Korea to effect the surrender of the sons of Nippon. To facilitate arrangements a demarcation line was fixed at the 38th Parallel. This imaginary line turned into a permanent border as all efforts to work out an independence agreement for the whole of Korea broke down. In 1947 an exasperated America handed over the problem to the United Nations. But Russia stubbornly refused to co-operate with the U.N. and so in August 1948 the Republic of Korea (ROK) was established under the presidency of Dr Syngman Rhee. A month later the Democratic People's Republic was formed in the North with Kim Il Sung, a former anti-Japanese guerrilla leader, as premier and Russian puppet.

It was an unhappy arrangement from the very beginning, with both halves of the country claiming jurisdiction over the whole peninsula. Sporadic fighting broke out along the 38th Parallel within months of the two republics coming into being. Alarms and excursions continued until 25 June 1950, when the Russian-trained North Korean Army launched a surprise offensive against the South.

Within hours of the North Korean tanks rolling out of the

* General Matthew Ridgway, an admirer of MacArthur and who was to succeed him as Supreme Commander in Korea, later condemned MacArthur in his book *The War in Korea* (Cresset Press, 1968) for not assessing the North Korean terrain, closing his ears to Chinese threats and scattering his forces in such a way that they were vulnerable to guerrilla harassment and encirclement.

mist and across the 38th Parallel the Chinese Communists came under suspicion as the instigators of the invasion. In fact, it has now been established beyond much doubt that the Russians were behind the initiative. But in 1950 the theory of a world-wide Communist conspiracy had spread throughout all the Western capitals, and China seemed an obviously guilty party to the military adventure. Subsequent investigation, however, has pointed to Stalin's being the prime mover behind the war.

The last of the occupying American troops had been withdrawn from Korea in 1949 and both the U.S. Secretary of State, Dean Acheson, and General MacArthur, then Supreme Commander of the Allied Powers in Japan, had gone on public record that South Korea was beyond the American defence perimeter in the Pacific. The Soviet Union and North Korea must have assumed, therefore, that America would not intervene in any war resulting from an attempted take-over of the South.

Moreoever, the Russians had their own reasons, other than just wishing to see a Communist-controlled country within the hegemony of the Soviet Union, for inspiring the invasion. With a united Korea firmly within its sphere of influence, Russia's own eastern defence perimeter would be considerably extended and made more secure, and Korea would then form a major segment of the ring which Stalin was attempting to draw round China. Although relations between the two giant Communist powers were ostensibly close and cemented with a treaty, there was a high degree of mutual distrust for a number of historical reasons. Stalin, looking to the future, wanted to neutralize China by fencing her in with Korea, Mongolia, Sinkiang and, possibly in the long term, Indo-China.

None of this was apparent, of course, in 1950, and in Washington the distant view across the Potomac was of hordes of yellow men, this time with red stars, again sweeping across Asia. The leaders in Peking were thought to be 'Stalinists' (an idea still held by some in President Kennedy's administration in the 'sixties) and out to extend their territory by war and revolution.

The truth of the matter was that Mao Tse-tung did not know of Russia's and North Korea's invasion plans, and it is now generally believed that it was only two days before the assault took place that he was informed of what was about to happen. As we have seen in the preceding chapter, China had enough problems on her hands in 1950–51 without getting herself unnecessarily engaged in a dubious initiative from which she could derive little or no benefit. Korea had been a Japanese colony since 1910, and China's contacts with the country were minimal, the North being under the firm and exclusive control of Moscow. In Red China's eyes Taiwan was the prime target, both from the military and the political point of view.

Indeed, in the early months of the war, China was a largely indifferent spectator of what was happening on the other side of the Manchurian border, although she naturally would not have been displeased at the initial Communist successes.

For their opening offensive the North Koreans used seven infantry divisions and one armoured. Their assault took the South by surprise in spite of earlier indications that something of the sort was being planned. The ROK units disintegrated under the hammer blows of these divisions which were backed by marauding squadrons of Yak fighters. Seoul, the southern capital, fell on 28 June, three days after the opening shots had been fired. By July, advance units of the Red Korean army were across the Han River, probing towards Taejon and the important port of Pusan.

President Truman reacted swiftly to the Korean crisis. First, he ordered General MacArthur to send arms and supplies to the ROK and then, as the position continued to deteriorate rapidly, he ordered in American ground forces. The first U.S. units arrived in Korea on 1 July; six days later they were in action. Meanwhile the U.N. Security Council recommended all members to furnish assistance to the South. The Soviet Union was absent from this meeting and therefore unable to use its veto as it undoubtedly would have done. Russia was going through one of its periodic sulks at the U.N., and Stalin clearly failed to anticipate the U.N response to the Korean crisis.

America's decision to go to the aid of South Korea flew in the face of the earlier declarations that the ROK was outside the American defence perimeter. A more serious reversal of policy

The Chinese Red Army

was President Truman's decision to order the 7th Fleet to patrol the Straits of Taiwan, which separate the island from China. This step was taken on strategic grounds, the Americans believing that it was essential to neutralize the island.

But only in January Truman had made it categorically clear that America intended to follow a policy of non-interference in Chinese affairs. He announced that the U.S. had no predatory designs on Taiwan or any other Chinese territory and added:

The United States has no desire to obtain special rights or privileges or to establish military bases on Formosa at this time. Nor does it have an intention of utilizing its armed forces to interfere in the present situation. The United States Government will not pursue a course which will lead to involvement in the civil conflict in China.

These were strong and unequivocal words. Dean Acheson supported the President by declaring: 'We are not going to get involved militarily in any way on the island of Formosa. So far as I know, no responsible person in the Government, no military man, has ever believed that we should involve our forces in the island.'

But now, four months later, the 7th Fleet was ordered into the Straits and America was committed to supporting Chiang Kai-shek. The Generalissimo was saved from his Communist enemies, China was intensely annoyed at what she considered a direct interference in her internal affairs, and the scene was set for a broader conflict in Korea. The Peking leaders deplored the American action, but confined themselves to harsh words. There was no immediate retaliation, but the alarm bells were ringing in military establishments all over the People's Republic. The first tentative preparations were made for putting the country on a war footing.

Against this political and diplomatic backcloth the Korean War increased in tempo and for both sides it became a race against time. The North Koreans realized they had to win quickly if they were going to win at all, and their objective was the port of Pusan. With Pusan in their hands they could prevent the U.N. forces going to the aid of the shattered South Koreans. The U.N. Command's immediate aim was to save Pusan, pour as

72

many troops as possible into Korea and build up a perimeter outside and around the port. MacArthur's men won the race, and in desperate and bloody fighting they blunted the North Korean spearhead. Strategic deadlock resulted. To break it, MacArthur devised and planned a seaborne invasion, two hundred miles behind the North Korean lines at a small town called Inchon. It was a brilliant stroke, superbly executed by U.S. Marines, and it brought about the disintegration of the North Korean Army. The Inchon landings were MacArthur's masterpiece; the victory should have crowned a great career. But the very success of the operation led him on to near-disaster as he pursued a broken enemy and vague political notions. All thoughts of a limited, localized war were now like so much drifting dust behind the advancing U.N. columns. The North Koreans, forced to break off the Pusan perimeter fight by the landings behind them, fell back in scattered groups towards their own half of the country and what they hoped would be a sanctuary.

But the Americans, with MacArthur as their mouthpiece, and many in the U.N., now saw an opportunity to create a united Korea, imposing a Western solution on an Asian problem. Mac-Arthur was readily given permission to extend his operations beyond the 38th Parallel and the rush began to the Yalu River and the Chinese border. Even now MacArthur may have been dreaming of taking the war to the Chinese and knocking out the new People's Republic before it had time to take root.

What MacArthur had in mind we shall never know. But what was on the mind of the Peking leadership became clear quickly enough; an advance into North Korea was unacceptable. To have the 7th Fleet cruising off the China coast was bad indeed, but the prospect of having U.N. troops on the Manchurian border was too much. Viewed from Peking, it seemed that the Western powers were trying to hem in China with a steel cordon. On 2 October, while the North Koreans were in headlong flight, Chou En-lai called the Indian Ambassador in Peking to a dramatic midnight meeting – Chou has always preferred the late hours for work and action – and told him in blunt terms that if American troops entered North Korea then China would have to resist them. The Indian Ambassador relayed the message but scant notice was taken even though China emphasized her position in a number of public declarations.

As China adopted a tough posture and started to send troops into Manchuria, Mao had the comforting knowledge that any military commitment would be supported by Russia. Stalin's miscalculation about American reactions to a Korean invasion had resulted in North Korea suffering a terrible defeat. Russia did not want to intervene directly as she was locked in the European cold war struggle, so she turned to China, to a Government which already believed itself in deadly peril from the West. Stalin agreed to supply the Chinese with tanks, artillery, aircraft and all manner of supplies and equipment if they went to war. In later years China was made to pay for every last item, but at the time the understanding was that this military aid would be free of charge.

While the Chinese were preparing to go to war, MacArthur was active on the political front and at a Wake Island meeting with President Truman he expressed the view that there was no danger of Mao sending in soldiers to help the defeated North Koreans. He told the President that he was confident of pushing on to the Yalu with only limited interruption from the Red rearguards. At this moment the first Chinese 'volunteers' were crossing the Yalu River for the pre-selected concentration points and, as we saw earlier, there were a number of sharp clashes between forward-U.N. and Chinese units.

But MacArthur said the Chinese would not fight, and that was that. On 24 November, in the face of all warnings, intelligence reports and rules of warfare, he launched his badly positioned troops in an offensive to end the war. Peace was expected by Christmas Day at the latest. But the attack hardly got going. On 26 November the Chinese launched their own general offensive. They struck with devastating effectiveness. The American 8th Army, knocked out of its forward stride, reeled and floundered. It came within an inch of being outflanked and encircled, but after some hard fighting and hard marching in the opposite direction to which it had moved on the 24th, the Chinese trap was avoided. Casualties were heavy, vast amounts of equipment and supplies were lost, and morale dipped to sub-zero. The U.S. Marines were surrounded by the Chinese, but their superior fighting qualities enabled them to punch through the encircling enemy and embark on a fighting retreat, an epic of courage and endurance which deservedly has a high place in the annals of the Marine Corps.

As the U.N. armies streamed back southward, their objective was promptly changed. The idea of uniting the whole of Korea was dropped with the same alacrity with which it had been taken up a few months earlier. December saw the U.N. forces being given back their original task – that of defending South Korea in a conventional war of limited aims.

With the broken forces of the U.N. streaming back to the 38th Parallel either in disorderly panic or with Marine Corps bearing, we can look at the Chinese armies and the men who by delivering so hard a knock to MacArthur's men had upset all the plans and hopes of the Commander-in-Chief and the Western politicians. The Chinese armies which overflowed in a roaring torrent into North Korea were different in a number of respects from those which had swamped the Nationalists in 1948–49. The defence pact between China and Russia, produced by Mao Tse-tung's visit to Moscow, had resulted in the dispatch to the PLA of more than 3000 Soviet Army officers, advisers and technicians. Their job was to re-organize and modernize the unwieldy PLA armies. The outbreak of the Korean War and the Chinese intervention interrupted their work. Nevertheless they were able to accomplish much.

Infantry divisions were increased in size and were given some support artillery, usually one battalion of twelve guns. Training in armoured tactics was started and attention was paid to co-operation between tanks and infantry. Training centres and academies for young officers were set up along with institutes for higher war studies, though these had hardly got going before their students were required at the front.

The PLA was slimmed of much of its excess, ideologically unsound weight, and discipline was considerably tightened. The long-term aim was to make the PLA a duplicate of the Russian Army, a plan disrupted by the Korean conflict and further retarded by the later Sino-Russian quarrel. And the Chinese had to go into Korea still heavily dependent on the rifle and bayonet, for the shortage of tanks and artillery was acute. The Russians never wholly fulfilled their promises to make good the deficiencies in tanks, guns and fighters, but this was due in part to the shortage of trained Chinese personnel to operate them. Training bases sprang up all over Manchuria but there were inevitably long delays before the cadres were ready to operate on the battlefield.

As the Korean war clouds drifted towards the Yalu River, the High Command assembled a force of some quarter of a million men in the Manchurian area, and in October Lin Piao, who had been given overall command, began to organize the ferrying of these men across the border and into remote and well-concealed staging areas. Peking announced the formation of a Chinese People's Volunteer Army (PVA), and the fiction of PLA soldiers in Korea being 'volunteers' was maintained throughout the war.

The PVA, as it must now be designated for the war's duration, shuttled units across the Yalu at a rapid pace, and as soon as they moved out of Manchuria others moved in from central and southern China. It has been estimated that by November there were 850,000 Chinese soldiers massed on both sides of the border.

These Chinese armies – individually they numbered anything between 10,000 and 20,000 men – were short of artillery, supply vehicles, signal equipment and medical services. Later in the war the Chinese were to suffer heavily because of these shortages. The High Command were aware of the dangers of going into battle against well-trained European troops while so seriously lacking in battlefield essentials. They gambled, however, on preponderance of numbers and surprise; and, anyway, had not the Russians agreed to make good what the PVA might need later?

Although the PVA relied heavily on the rifle and bayonet, many units had not enough even of these to arm every man. In some regiments only one man in five had a rifle. The others carried large numbers of grenades. They were expected to arm themselves with captured enemy weapons. The PVA was well

76

supplied, however, with mortars, which the Chinese used intelligently and effectively.

The offensive of 26 November was launched with fourteen divisions. The plan was simple enough: to swamp the over-extended U.N. positions and outflank its armies. It almost succeeded. The fact that the attack was launched in the depths of winter demonstrates the confidence of the Chinese commanders both in their men and in their ability to achieve surprise and seize the initiative. This confidence was not misplaced. The Chinese hit hard, usually attacked from an unexpected quarter and continually probed for the flank; they moved at incredible speed through the most difficult snow covered country and, while keeping up the pressure along a wide front, put in a series of unending left and right hooks which bewildered the dazed U.N. forces.

For a brief while it looked as if the whole U.N. Army would go into the Chinese 'bag'. That it didn't was partly owing to the fighting qualities displayed by a number of units, to some outstanding lower-order generalship and to U.N. air power; moreover, the Chinese were unable to follow up quickly as the U.N. Army broke clear because of their lack of transport and the consequent slow delivery of supplies. The firepower which the U.N. soldiers had been able to put down had also surprised and dismayed some Chinese divisions. Here their experience against the Nationalists told against them. They were quite used to artillery and machine-gun fire, but not to fire directed and co-ordinated as it was in Korea. The Red Chinese had become used to brief barrages and a concerted rush at the Nationalists' positions. Their demoralized opponents had rarely put up a stubborn defence. These easy victories led commanders and soldiers alike into over-confidence, and although much the same tactics were initially successful in Korea the loss in men was heavy. Lin Piao had to call up fresh divisions to replace some of his more battered ones.

The U.N. forces had fallen back to near the 38th Parallel where a defensive line had been formed. They were given a brief breathing space and a few precious days to prepare the line for the inevitable attack. Considering the distance the PVA had to cover, mostly on foot, and their considerable casualties, it is remarkable that they were able to deploy against the line before the end of December. On New Year's Day, to the usual cacophony of bugle calls and hysterical screaming, the Chinese hurled themselves forward in 'human waves', a manner which was to become familiar, but the frequency of which was then and later exaggerated, throughout the campaign. Wave after wave of infantry slammed into the U.N. positions until these were either overrun or cut off. This saturation approach to warfare again worked; the defensive line bent and then had to be re-adjusted further south. On 4 January the 'volunteers' entered Seoul, the third time the capital had changed hands during the war.

The Chinese kept up the pressure of their offensive for three weeks; but then the cost in men and equipment became too heavy, momentum was lost and the attacks petered out. Massive U.N. firepower again took its toll, and the Chinese had little heavy artillery with which to reply. The 'volunteers' also endured heavy blows from U.N. fighter and bomber squadrons which attacked rear communications and supply dumps.

For reasons never explained Lin Piao now relinquished his command. He may have been ill, or possibly exhausted by the tempo of his own blitz campaign. It has been surmised that he may have been wounded in the January offensive. Whatever the reason, Lin left Korea with his reputation enhanced; his feat of moving a large army into North Korea and keeping it more or less undetected under the noses of his opponents was alone sufficient to justify him a high place among Chinese commanders of real ability and quality.

Lin's successor was Peng Teh-huai, whom we last met in Sinkiang Province as the Tibet invasion got under way. Peng, who had once served as a brigadier with the Nationalists, was a tough, stubborn soldier, noted for his rough tongue and coarse habits. No sooner had he assumed command than he was faced with a crisis. The U.N. forces had by now largely recovered from the shock and manpower punch of the Chinese offensives. They had taken the measure of the Chinese; they no longer underestimated them, but there was a general feeling that they could not only be stopped, they could be beaten. Morale had visibly improved, there was no more talk about 'buggin' out', and the first grim jokes about Chinese 'hordes' were to be heard – 'I saw three, shot two and captured the other.' With their spirit improved and with strong reinforcements, the U.N. High Command felt able to undertake a counterstroke. It was launched in February just as Peng took over from Lin.

The Chinese fought doggedly to hold on to their recent hard-won gains. Peng made frequent tours of the front to inspire his men and was often under fire. But with only small arms, the volunteers were unable to hold off the spirited U.N. attacks. They had little with which to fight the tank spearheads and their artillery was too thinly spread to be of much assistance to the men in the weapon pits. The PVA casualties were enormous, and one by one their defensive positions had to be evacuated. Seoul was given up on 14 March. The fighting went on until the end of the month. It was sustained and bitter, the U.N. pressure unrelenting and the Chinese refusing to give up an inch of territory without a stiff fight. But slowly the Chinese fell back, unable to withstand the perpetual bombardment from artillery, tanks and aircraft. The slogging match came to an end as March gave way to April and the first forgiving signs of spring showed themselves over the bleak and desolate landscape. Both sides were exhausted by the scale, intensity and duration of the struggle. The PVA had been able to establish a new line on the North Korean side of the 38th Parallel, and there it was given a short respite and a quiet interlude to re-group and re-organize.

Then, on 11 April 1951, the Chinese gained their biggest political success of the Korean War. On that date President Truman announced that General MacArthur had been dismissed. Mac-Arthur, who after the brilliant success of the Inchon landings had become too high and mighty, had committed a fatal mistake for any senior officer: he got himself involved in politics, he over-estimated his own popularity and the weight his views carried; and he seriously underestimated the strength and courage of Truman. MacArthur had argued that the Chinese would not intervene in Korea. When this view proved wrong, he urged that the U.N. air force should be allowed to attack Manchuria, which he described as a 'privileged sanctuary' from which Chinese and North Korean MiGs could operate. But the General went further than debating his point with his political superiors. He appealed to the American public through the press, which he assiduously courted as a means of getting his opinions across.

After his dismissal, the General, in a speech to Congress, advocated a tougher and more forward strategy against China. It included an economic blockade, the possible use of Nationalist troops on Taiwan against the mainland, and the authorizing of the U.N. High Command to extend aerial surveillance over Manchuria and other parts of China – half a step away from bombing these areas. MacArthur clearly wanted a showdown with China, but for the Truman administration the risks were far too great, the brinkmanship far too much of a strain. Not least was the danger of America's becoming involved in war on two fronts – with the Russians in Europe and the Chinese in the Far East. MacArthur had wanted to go too far, and although he was popular at home his subsequent speeches and a Senate inquiry not only justified Truman in public and swung majority opinion to his side, but warned Americans in particular of the dangers of allowing generals too much power and room for political manoeuvre. General Omar Bradley, chairman of the Joint Chiefs of Staff, described MacArthur's strategy for conflict with China as 'the wrong war, at the wrong place, at the wrong time and with the wrong enemy'. It was an apt summary.

But though the fight against the Chinese was not going to be carried to the mainland, there was no question of calling a halt in Korea. The fighting there continued with unabated ferocity. Since taking over from Lin, Peng had been forced to fight on the defensive and in doing so had absorbed some lessons from the U.N. offensives. He decided to go over to the attack, but before doing so he re-organized his artillery, concentrating it for pre-assault bombardments. He had also been reinforced with some new divisions from Manchuria, and the trickle of Russian tanks from the Yalu steadily increased. By mid-April he was ready to unleash his assault divisions. The attack went in briskly and the

A PLA section on duty on the Great Wall of China in 1937, just before the war with
an.

Non-combatant peasants made themselves useful to the PLA in its struggles with the
omintang by organizing the transport of food to the front line. This picture was taken
re than 30 years ago, but the PLA's transport system is still run on much the same
s in many remote areas.

3. A Cecil Beaton study of a 'Surprise Soldier' (commando) from his book *The Years Between*.

4. The PLA enters Peking. Banner-waving citizens welcome the Red Army as it marches into the capital during the final stages of the Civil War.

5. Prisoners of Chiang Kai-shek, these Communist soldiers were captured during the first ill-fated attempt to seize Hainan Island from the Nationalists.

6. April, 1950: Assault troops practise a beach landing on Hainan Island for the projected invasion of Taiwan (Formosa). The plan was overtaken by the Korean War.

7. Major General Edward Almond, U.S. Tenth Corps Commander, questions a Chinese prisoner through an interpreter.

8. 'Don't shoot!' These prisoners had apparently been told by their officers that the Americans would shoot them if they were captured.

9. November, 1950: Some of the first Chinese prisoners to be captured by the Americans in North Korea.

10. A PLA officer briefs a North Korean officer before handing over command of his section of the defensive line near the 38th Parallel.

11. PLA soldiers, captured by U.S. Marines soon after Chinese intervention in the Korea War, find shelter from the bitter wind against a rock face.

. Going home! Chinese soldiers rejoice with North Koreans at the news that they are
ing back to Manchuria. The last of the PLA units withdrew from North Korea in 1958.

. A farewell salute. PLA men ceremonially take their leave of their Korean hillside
nker near the ceasefire line.

14. A youthful-looking Lin Piao; a picture taken in the 1950s.

15. Lin Piao in his 'regalia' of a Marshal of the PLA. A photograph taken shortly befor ranks and insignia were abolished.

16. A 1951 march-past. The men are wearing Russian-style combat smocks.

17. Wearing their new-style uniforms with forage caps, PLA men raise their arms and chant slogans in support of Mao's 1958 hard-line approach to Taiwan.

18. Tanks and their crews on parade in Peking in 1957.

19. An impressive display of light tanks in Peking's 'Red Square' during the early 'fifties.

20. PLA tank crews line up for inspection in an exercise area south of Peking.

21. Weapons inspection. The PLA pays more attention to weapon training than sartorial elegance.

. Mao's Thoughts for the peasants – the official Chinese news agency says this
hotograph depicts PLA men bringing Mao's Thoughts and portrait to the peasants to
lighten them and promote agriculture.

. In support of Mao – soldiers stationed on Hainan Island write poster slogans in praise
the Chairman.

. A 1951 display of force to mark the 30th anniversary of the foundation of the
ommunist Party.

. The war with India. Chinese troops marching over the Yingko (Eagle's Nest) Pass to
ke up positions on the Tanchiapani River.

26. A jovial Mao Tse-tung, leader of 700 million people.

27. Mao with his old friend, the late Edgar Snow, who was the first journalist to interview Mao in 1936 when he was a struggling revolutionary. His subsequent book, *Red Star Over China*, is a classic and a primary source on Mao's early days and those of the P.L.A. Lin Piao holds on to a work of greater renown but dubious long-term merit – the *Little Red Book* of Mao's Thoughts.

28. Liu Shao-chi, who was under attack by the Red Guards when this picture was taken, and Chou En-lai, China's permanent Mandarin. Unlike Liu, he survived the upheaval of the Cultural Revolution.

29. The Cultural Revolution took away the smiles of some old Party members – left to right, Chu Teh, Madame Soong Ching-ling (the widow of Dr Sun Yat-sen), Head-of-state (soon to be deposed) Liu Shao-chi. Chou En-lai has his back to the camera.

30. Chu Teh, founding father of the People's Liberation Army.

Chairman Mao and Defence Minister Lin Piao at a Peking rally during the Cultural
volution. They are wearing the new drab olive uniforms with which the PLA was
ued after 1965.

A break in training for a test on the manual – not the *Little Red Book* for this is a
7 picture.

On patrol in Shanghai. When this picture was taken the PLA was beginning to exert
influence for a return to order after the excesses of the Cultural Revolution.

It looks more like a scene from a
:ond-rate film than a battle exercise, but
s official picture from the Hsinhua
ency claims to depict the latter.
thusiastic buglers are essential members
PLA infantry units.

Close comrades-in-arms? Mao and Lin
eive the acclamation of PLA soldiers,
t when this picture was taken in 1970 the
o men were already deadly rivals behind
scenes for the leadership of China.

The soldier is a girl – Hu Yi-ling, a
mber of the PLA, was studying
oanese at Peking University when this
ture was taken in 1972.

底粉碎中国的林 彪 晓夫 的新反

彻底粉碎
中国赫鲁晓夫！

7. 'Hurrah for Mao' and 'Down with Liu Shao-chi'. These are said to be the sentiments
ed soldiers are expressing at a rally in Inner Mongolia. Liu, the Head-of-State, was
enounced as 'China's Krushchev' and was removed from office.

3. New recruits to the PLA listen to a between-training chat on what the red star stands
or.

9. Border guards on duty in August, 1969. Chinese characters on the board say: 'Never
low violation of the Chinese territory, Chen Pao Island'.

40. PLA men stand guard outside the Soviet Embassy in Peking as anti-Russian sentiment spreads through the capital after the border fighting.

41. A photograph released by Peking's Hsinhua Agency of a border guard argument on the frozen Ussuri. The caption said that after the Chinese reasoned with the 'invaders', the Russians, having a 'guilty conscience and unjust cause', put their vehicles into reverse.

2. The Ussuri River and Damansky Island. Triangle and circle indicate areas where clashes have occurred between Chinese and Russian frontier guards.

3. A view from the other side. Soviet soldiers are given a final briefing before setting out on patrol along a disputed area of the Ussuri River in March, 1969.

4. Militiamen in Kwangchow raise their arms during a mass rally to denounce the 'sanguinary crime of Soviet revisionist encroachment upon China's territory' in March, 1969.

5. Chinese guards, their backs to the camera, argue with their Russian counterparts. Such scenes were common in 1969 and both sides released pictures of incidents as part of the wider propaganda battle.

6. A PLA patrol moves out along the banks of the Amur River.

7. A rough-house on the ice. Swinging their weapons and throwing snowballs the Chinese 'attack' Russians on Damansky Island.

48. Russian guards seem unperturbed by this border demonstration. But the Chinese, this time, are only armed with pictures of Mao and copies of his Thoughts.

49. Among the dead – Russian Army Colonel D. V. Leonov was killed on 15 March 19 fighting on the disputed Damansky Island. Russian sources said Leonov had been a candidate in the local council elections and a blood-covered copy of his victory speech was found in a pocket of his uniform.

50. Going on leave? PLA men in the waiting room at White Cloud Airport in Canton. Picture by Frank Fischbeck.

51. PLA soldiers, in their ceremonial uniforms, on parade at Peking Airport for the arrival of President Nixon on 21 February, 1972.

52. Keng Yu-chi, Deputy Commander of the 196th Infantry Division, and a hero of the Korean War. He is seen here talking of his Division's exploits during the Civil War and in Korea when journalists visited his headquarters at Yuang, 60 miles east of Peking, in February, 1972.

53. Members of the 196th Infantry Division hold up their targets as part of the drill before a shooting exhibition, laid on for foreign journalists covering President Nixon's China trip. A Denes Baracs photograph.

54. Review order for President Nixon's inspection.

Chinese made some gains, but unknown to Peng the U.N. Command had also been planning an offensive. The Chinese blows were parried or absorbed and then the U.N. offensive went in as a counter-attack.

The PVA was surprised and thrown off balance, many of their commanders being incapable of mental re-adjustment. Lack of signals equipment also probably told against the Chinese; some units were obviously in two minds as to whether to attack or defend. This lack of communication between divisions and High Command made it difficult for commanders to adjust their plans once their men were committed. There was no battlefield flexibility. The Chinese stuck rigidly to their allotted tasks simply because there was rarely any means, other than by messenger, to tell them to do otherwise. However, Peng managed to bring order out of battle chaos. It took him two weeks and cost him some ground and, as always a high toll of lives. But a great deal was needed to daunt Peng, who at the best of times was none too imaginative. On 16 May he ordered yet another attack, and this time it went in with the infantry displaying a fanatical bravery over and above anything seen before on the Korean hills. Wave after wave of them went down before the swathing machine-guns, while artillery pounded the forming-up areas in the rear. Fighters swarmed like disturbed hornets over the front strafing and napalm bombing. But nothing, it seemed, could stop these Chinese. They just kept on going. Peng's casualties were enormous with some divisions suffering at least fifty per cent losses. The U.N. front wilted and then was pushed back to a depth of about fifteen miles.

Peng pressed on too long and too hard. His losses all but catastrophic, he had eventually to call a respite. And this was the chance the U.N. Command had been waiting for. Sensing the utter exhaustion of the Chinese and giving them no time to consolidate their newly won positions, the U.N. once more counter-attacked, evicting the PVA back over the 38th Parallel. The last major land battle was over.

The months from November 1950, to June 1951 saw battles of an awesomeness more usually associated with the First World War, artillery barrages of an intensity last seen in the Western desert and on the Russian front. But still, in the main, it was an infantryman's war, attack and counter-attack, close-quarter fighting at its most terrifying. It was to remain an infantryman's war after June; but it was war of a different sort. Both sides dug in, fortified their positions and settled down to morale-sapping, nerve-straining trench warfare. For the next two years the war was one of patrolling, skirmishing, raiding and artillery duels.

The winter and spring battles of 1950–51 had left both sides exhausted, but the Chinese more so. Their commanders could no longer afford to mount the massive infantry assaults which had marked the days since the PVA's intervention. Even for China, manpower was not limitless and resources had to be husbanded. North Korea had been 'freed', there was now little danger of the war being carried into China proper, and with the front stabilized, further offensives were not strictly necessary. The U.N. losses in men had also been heavy, the majority among Americans who had taken the brunt of the war, but they were nothing like those suffered by the PVA and the North Korean Army. The freeing of South Korea from the Communists allowed the U.N Command also to forgo further general offensives and in November 1951, General Ridgway, who had taken over from MacArthur, ordered General Van Fleet to entrench and begin an 'active defence' along what became known as the Kansas-Wyoming line.

The war was a stalemate with honours just about even, and the immediate objective of both sides became the domination of no-man's-land. All wars are said to be subalterns' wars, but this became especially true of Korea after June 1951, as day and night patrols and raiding parties went out. Sometimes local clashes escalated into battles of regimental strength, but these were the exception. In the terrible heat of summer and the zero temperatures of winter a dirty, unforgiving war raged between the barbed wire and sandbags of the opposing lines.

As the pattern of the struggle changed, ceasefire feelers began to be put out. The opening move came from the Russians. Jacob Malik, the Soviet ambassador to the U.N. first suggested that a ceasefire should be negotiated, and after much communication behind the scenes between all the parties, two delegations met for purely military talks on 8 July at Kaesong, near the 38th Parallel.

Hopes were raised by these discussions. Unduly as it turned out; the war was not to end so easily. It quickly became apparent that the Communists were using the talks as a further extension of the ideological war between Communism and the West.

However, contact was maintained and the venue for the truce talks was moved from Kaesong to a little village on the road to Seoul. It was called Panmunjom, where for nearly two years the arguments went back and forth. There was progress and then deadlock. At one moment peace was thought to be within grasp, the next it was as far away as ever. One of the big sticking points was the question of the repatriation of prisoners. Some 14,000 of the 20,000 Chinese prisoners and 36,000 of the 112,000 North Korean prisoners did not want to go back to their respective countries. The Communists could not agree to this as it would constitute a major political victory for the U.N powers; they insisted on compulsory repatriation. By sticking to this and other so-called principles the Communists hoped to wear down the resolution of the U.N. and gain a propaganda victory by default. It was then that the Reds introduced into their catalogue of denunciations of their opponents charges of germ warfare and atrocities against prisoners.

Then events outside Korea brought a change of climate at Panmunjom. In November 1952, General Eisenhower was elected President of the United States. Among his campaign promises was a pledge to bring an end to the Korean fighting. Eisenhower let it be known in Peking that if progress was not made towards an armistice then America would consider widening the war taking it into Manchuria and using atomic weapons. MacArthur must have winced.

Of greater impact, so far as the Communists were concerned, was the death of Stalin in March 1953. This was followed by a general improvement of international relations which quickly showed itself at the peace talks. Suddenly there was co-operation, even on the vital question of prisoners. The rapid progress made after Stalin's death is an indication of who had thitherto been calling the tune on Korea. June saw a compromise, but close enough to the U.N. stand not to matter. The Chinese and North Koreans who did not want to go back were to be handed over to a repatriation committee made up of representatives from neutral nations. This question out of the way, the path to peace was clear. On 27 July 1953, the war ended with the signing of an armistice. But Chinese and American troops glared at each other across the border for five more years until late in 1958, when the last of the PVA volunteers withdrew to Manchuria.

The cost to all sides in men and treasure had been high. The Chinese and North Koreans were estimated by the U.N. Command to have sustained between one-and-a-half and two million casualties, while a million Koreans from both North and South civilian populations died. American casualties numbered 142,000 and there were a further 17,000 among the other U.N. forces.

But the Chinese manpower losses on the battlefields do not tell the whole story. The casualties on the home front were even greater. When the Korean War broke out there was still a large reservoir of pro-American feeling in the Chinese main population centres, and in some quarters there were serious doubts as to the wisdom of the PLA engaging in a conflict with the U.S. Mao stamped hard on these doubters as part of his programme for uniting the country behind the war effort. There was a sharp increase in terror and coercion against all 'counter-revolutionaries' and it has been estimated that in the first six months of 1951 between one and three million people were executed while millions of others were sent to labour camps for 're-education'. It was a heavy price to pay for unification behind the red star, but cheaper than that paid in other and smaller Communist states.

The war produced not only political and human stress at home, but also a considerable economic strain, owing to the heavy demands made on industry by the insatiable war machine. It has been said, and with truth, that the Korean conflict helped to unite China and gave the Red leaders an opportunity of consolidating their position. At the same time it generated a great deal of internal conflict which in turn led to severe repression and put an almost insupportable burden on an economy that was still in tatters from the civil war and Japanese occupation. Only Soviet assistance, which led to an unwelcome dependence, saved it from total collapse.

But China made some positive gains from the war. She achieved her military objective of keeping American troops away from her border and in doing so established herself as a major power in the eyes of the Communist bloc. On the debit side, China lost any chance of taking Taiwan, and for twenty years her relations with America were poisoned and embittered, the effects of which had world-wide repercussions.

The Korean War was one which neither side really won or lost. But one fringe participant, and the cause of all the trouble, did lose considerably. Russia's assistance to China and North Korea put her own economy under severe strain, and she was forced to turn to Eastern Europe for help. The demands made upon these Soviet-dominated countries resulted in internal stresses which produced the revolts of the 'fifties. At the same time the Atlantic Alliance was given fresh impetus and consequently strengthened with the addition of West Germany. Japan was also placed firmly and cosily under the American defensive umbrella. The lessons went home where they mattered in the Kremlin, and the Soviet Union has been extremely chary of further initiatives on the Korean pattern.

How did the Chinese People's Liberation Army come out of all this? The answer is 'Chastened but by no means demoralized'. Casualties were certainly high but the Army had attained its goal, it had stood up well against a better-armed opponent and had fought with a bravery and *élan* which had at first surprised every one of its opponents.

The Chinese generals have been accused by some Western commentators of being prodigal with their men's lives, of behaving like First World War commanders in their lack of imagination and initiative. There is some truth in these charges. After the brilliant opening gambit of secreting a quarter of a million men in North Korea and following it up with a lightning blitz for checkmate, Chinese generalship certainly deteriorated. But there are reasons. Brought up on the doctrines of guerrilla and mobile warfare, the Red commanders found themselves cramped and restricted in the narrow Korean peninsula and could find no cure for their strategical claustrophobia. Accustomed to the wide open spaces of China with ample room for deployment and manoeuvre, the Chinese took a long time to come to terms with the nature of the country in which they were fighting. Another point, but an important one, is that for the first time the Red commanders were operating in an alien country, their troops moving among a largely hostile population (even in the North the Chinese were not too well received); their knowledge of the terrain was limited, their maps usually inadequate and often inaccurate. These are problems which any commander might expect to encounter in war, but for the Chinese they had added significance since most Chinese do not like fighting away from their homeland and rarely understand the logic of why they should be called upon to do so; consequently, their performance suffers. The Chinese in Korea, however, overcame this psychological handicap rather more quickly than a study of their military history might have suggested.

The real stumbling block for the Chinese was the linear warfare imposed by General Ridgway. Unable to manoeuvre, the only answer the commanders could come up with was the 'human wave' attack by which they hoped to pierce and then swamp the wired, mined and artillary-supported line. These tactics had worked against the shaky Nationalists towards the end of the civil war, but in Korea they proved costly and futile against properly fortified positions from which concentrated firepower could be summoned up. The courage of the Red soldiers was incredible, at times indeed fanatical, and they did achieve local successes. But what did not work in Flanders in 1914–18 certainly could not work in Korea in 1951.

Their success with the overflow method at the start of the campaign led the Chinese to think the U.N. troops would repeatedly break under the weight of their attacks. But circumstances changed rapidly. In the Yalu River area the U.N. troops had been badly deployed and had got themselves into a situation which invited attack. But after the border shambles, when they had recovered their nerve and fighting spirit, established a firm line with secure flanks, and amassed a preponderance of artillery, tanks and aircraft, the Chinese found themselves up against the impossible.

The mass infantry attack was all that was left to the Red commanders. They had no capability for seaborne hooks and insufficient firepower to punch holes in the linear defence. But they did have men, hundreds of thousands of them, who were prepared and willing to run at the guns. But the supply was not inexhaustible, although it may have appeared so to the U.N. troops in the line; and provision for the wounded was almost totally lacking. New drafts had to be continually called upon from Manchuria, but the scythe in front of the lines cut them down as soon as they arrived. There was no alternative; a halt had to be called.

It should be pointed out here that although the Chinese used the 'human wave' method of warfare on many occasions, these were not as frequent as reporters at the time made out. Every Chinese attack was described in terms of 'hordes' and 'waves of infantry'. But subsequent research by historians of units taking part in the war has found that the PVA were comparatively sparing in their use of this method, usually reserving it for the big push on a wide front.

The Chinese learnt from their mistakes, and quickly diagnosed their problems. The need for extra firepower was obvious, and Peng Teh-huai went to considerable lengths to overcome this shortage. He increased the number of guns per division and in his later offensives concentrated them at selected points. But he was dependent on the Russians for artillery and they were slow in supplying him. He never had enough. To try to fill the gaps, he used his tanks in the role of mobile gun platforms, bringing them forward to support the infantry for localized attacks, but rarely letting them go right on with the attackers. It was an unsatisfactory solution. Despite their limitations the Chinese gunners performed well; they were both enthusiastic and adaptable, their counter-battery fire drawing admiring comment from American gunners. Like most Asian troops, they were able to get their guns into positions which Westerners would have written off as inaccessible or too dangerous. But then, when the stakes have seemed worth while, the Chinese have always been prepared to gamble.

The PVA's competence and courage, its early successes and stubbornness in adversity, not only disconcerted the U.N. forces but led them to search for excuses in which they were aided and abetted by the press, propaganda and publicity machines of those Allied powers who had troops at the battlefront. The excuses usually centred on some form of sneaky Orientalism; either the Chinese were cunning and full of deception, or they were callous, insensitive and prepared to see thousands of their men mown down. Whatever the Chinese did was somehow wrong, not the game as it should be played. The inference was they were winning, or at least not losing, because they were not abiding by the rules. They had no right to run at machine-guns in their thousands and die in their thousands. The rules and regulations had been changed and up-dated since Flanders.

Dennis Bloodworth* puts the Western attitude in a nutshell when he writes:

> The helter-skelter withdrawal of the American forces [from the Yalu] was perfectly comprehensible since they were 'swamped by a yellow tide'. When the British charged the German machine-guns at Ypres, they were heroes; when the Chinese charged in Korea, a number of unappetizing little explanations were cooked up. They were doped, 'hopped up with opium', said some. No, said others, they did not have to be doped because the Chinese nervous system was not finely co-ordinated like ours, and therefore their crude mechanism could not register our more delicate sentiments (like blue funk). They were in fact, sub-human, and the mass frontal assault was the only tactic they knew. Their nervous insensibility accounted for their cruelty, for they did not really feel pain, so, of course, being cruel to them was not like being cruel to you or me. . . .

In his suicidal frontal assaults on entrenched positions, the Chinese infantryman may have been considerably less than

* *Chinese Looking Glass*, p. 285.

imaginative, but he was certainly no coward. He fought and died in the only way he knew, the way he had been trained; his skin may have been yellow, but it gave him neither more nor less protection than a white skin from the searing bullets; he suffered neither more nor less than a U.N. soldier when hit by flying lead and burning shrapnel; he suffered as much as a white man from hunger pains, frost-bite and the blazing sun, and he was just as afraid to die and scared of being seen to be afraid. Unlike the U.N. soldier, however, he died more frequently and complained less.

One of the best descriptions of the bravery of the Chinese infantryman is given by Michael Elliott-Bateman in his book *Defeat in the East*. He relates a story told by a non-commissioned officer who had served in Korea:

He described a Chinese attack that came in over a ridge, down a steep gully, and up on to his hill position. He said, 'As they came over the ridge our artillery caught them and prevented their effective withdrawal. Down in the gully our mortars rained death on them and the American planes flew up and down the gully frying them with napalm. As they came up our hill they were caught in our concentrated machine-gun cross-fire.' In the pause I asked what happened and he replied, 'Well, of course they took our position, but we knocked hell out of them.' These were assault troops.

And again, Mr Bateman writes of a conversation he had with a British company commander who had faced Chinese frontal assaults – 'He told me that the problem was trigger fatigue. The trigger finger became exhausted with killing, and his men finished up by pulling the triggers of their weapons with the third, fourth, and little fingers.'

Many British and American soldiers who served in Korea relate similar stories, and those who helped to repel Chinese attacks or broke before them usually tell of the same feeling of nausea and mind-numbing horror at the killing, the steadily mounting heaps of bodies in front of their positions. But only those who have not come up against the Chinese soldier scoff at his courage and ability. In Korea he won the most that any soldier can expect to win from an opponent – his respect.

When for political and strategic reasons the war became a stagnant one of patrolling, raiding and unending reconnaissance, both sides claimed to have won the battle for the domination of no-man's-land. Whatever was the truth, the Red soldier proved himself to be a wily foe, able to move quickly and quietly at night and a dangerous opponent in the brief, savage skirmishes which erupted between the wire. In the days of the general offensives, he had been accused of a lack of initiative; in the days of the patrol war he was discovered to be endowed with an abundance of this quality. He certainly displayed it in his night work against the U.N. forward positions.

During the failure of the last Chinese push, a great many prisoners were taken by the U.N. forces, and subsequently there was a lot of publicity about the numbers of Chinese who did not wish to be repatriated. For political reasons, a great deal was made of this, and naturally so. But some explanation is needed of a situation in which a soldier can fight bravely for his country one minute and refuse to be returned to it the next. What had happened was that the PVA losses in the best-trained and most highly motivated units had been so heavy that Peng Teh-huai was forced to conserve the remaining ones. The new drafts from Manchuria were not in the same class as those who had gone before. The majority had been given only a few weeks' basic training before being sent to the front; many of them were ex-Nationalist soldiers of dubious loyalty to the Communist cause.

Peng used these ill-trained reinforcements to spearhead some of his attacks. These were the men who often went down in their thousands before the automatics and artillery of the U.N. troops. They were cannon fodder in the truest sense of that expression; often they were armed with just a few grenades, and those with rifles sometimes did not even know how to use them. These were the men who often brought about trigger fatigue among their opponents. When they had carried out their work of sapping enemy spirit and morale with their death-inviting advances, the PVA's quality troops took over and went in to storm the presumably exhausted defenders.

Out of these tactics grew the stories and legends that many Chinese went into the attack either drunk or driven by the whips of their officers. And no doubt there were cases of this in some units. Generally, however, these men did what was asked of them with Asian fatalism, but since their heart was never truly in the cause either of Communism or of freeing North Korea, they were not unduly downcast at being taken prisoner. Later, given the chance to go to Taiwan, many of them accepted it gladly.

By the time the days of patrolling and raiding arrived, the PVA was a considerably toughened Army and prisoners were not so easy to come by; neither were they quite so docile. The cannon fodder had been used up, and those who remained where battle-hardened, politically indoctrinated.

These, then, were the men who fought the troops of fifteen different nations all temporarily aligned under the U.N. flag. Poorly fed, often badly armed, without adequate artillery, rarely able to call down air strikes, without support from a navy, the Chinese soldier fought his own version of freedom's battle on the miserable hills of Korea. It was an inglorious war with victory eluding both sides; but to the Chinese way of thinking, he who does not lose wins.

WAR WITH INDIA: 1962

It is impossible to entertain the absurd idea
that our two great friendly nations with a
combined population of one thousand million
might start a war over such temporary and
local disputes – *Peking note to New Delhi*

China went to war with India on 20 October 1962. Her armies
struck with sudden but calculated fury from the border heights of
the North-East Frontier Agency and routed the Indians in their
path. Over in the West, in the Ladakh area, the Chinese ran into
stiffer opposition but nevertheless quickly gained their objectives.
It was a lightning campaign, brilliant in execution, dramatic and
devastating in impact and results.

And then, with the PLA divisions positioned and poised for a
thrust into the plains of Assam, with a mixture of panic and do-
or-die spirit beginning to grip the Indian peoples, the Chinese
abruptly called off the war. They announced a unilateral ceasefire
with effect from midnight of 21 November, and on 1 December
they began to withdraw their forces 'to positions 20 kilometres
behind the lines of actual control which existed between China and
India on 7 November 1959'. This was by any standards an extraordinary end to an already extraordinary and undeclared war. The
Chinese behaviour was unprecedented. Here was a nation giving
up voluntarily, and without the asking, all that it had claimed,
contested and won at a not inconsiderable cost. It was an astonishing gesture which bemused both their foes and their friends. But it
was no less astonishing that China and India, Asia's most popu-
lous nations and friends of very long standing, should have come
to blows at all.

Their quarrel, which resulted in the PLA blitzkrieg, rumbled on
in low key throughout the 1950s; its history, as might be expected,
is long and tortuous. But in its essentials the dispute was and is
relatively simple. In the Ladakh region China laid claim to the

92

Aksai Chin area, a bleak and desolate desert – 'Aksai Chin' means 'Desert of White Stones' – with hardly an inhabitant. Historically, India's claim to this inhospitable emptiness which can sustain neither man nor beast was stronger than that of the Chinese. But after independence in 1947 India had not bothered about the area and neglected to take physical possession of it. Why should she? On the maps in New Delhi it was marked as belonging to India, but it was of no earthly use. It was just one of those barren wastes that are so common a feature of Central Asian geography.

After the Chinese took over Tibet in 1950, the PLA found that the Aksai Chin was strategically indispensable for consolidating their hold on Tibet and also on Sinkiang Province, an area the Russians were reluctant to let go. The Chinese engineers moved in and built a military highway across the desert to link Sinkiang with Gartok in Western Tibet. This road enabled the Red Army to move supplies and men to any threatened area in half the time it took along the traditional caravan routes or by their limited number of transport aircraft. The highway, discovered by the Indians only in the late 1950s, some time after it had been built and was in operation, had become a vital PLA artery and there was clearly no question of the Chinese Government's giving it up. Its discovery intensely annoyed the Indian Government and, more important, large sections of the Indian public when it became general knowledge.

In the East the disputed border ran along the North-East Frontier Agency (NEFA). Here the Chinese had a much stronger case for re-adjustment of the frontier, but they did not press the matter. But the Indians regarded NEFA as of the same strategic importance to them as the Aksai Chin was to the Chinese. The territory is tribal country, mountainous and thickly wooded. In the valleys and lower regions there is thick jungle. The Indian Government took the Agency's border with China to be the McMahon Line although it had never been demarcated on the ground either by the British, who were responsible for the drawing of the line, or by the Indians.

India's frontier problems were an inheritance from the British Raj. The British had been somewhat arbitrary in drawing boundaries,

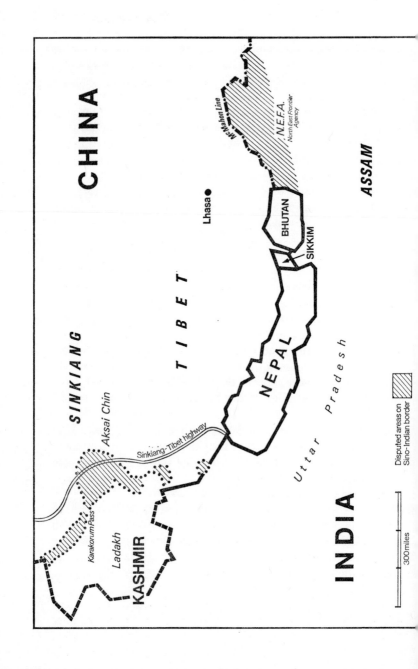

CHINA

SINKIANG

Aksai Chin

Sinkiang-Tibet highway

Karakorum Pass

Ladakh

KASHMIR

T I B E T

Lhasa ●

Uttar Pradesh

NEPAL

SIKKIM

BHUTAN

McMahon Line

N.E.F.A.
North East Frontier
Agency

ASSAM

INDIA

300 miles

Disputed areas on
Sino-Indian border

or, more often, pencilling lines on maps, to denote the limits of their interests. In the case of India's China borders, the British had hardly bothered to consult the Chinese, and Peking, no matter who was ruling at the time, had agreed to nothing. After independence the Indian Government accepted the British boundaries as *de facto*. Not unnaturally the new Communist Government in Peking adopted a different attitude: frontiers should be re-negotiated.

Some of India's claims in NEFA were dubious at best; the Tawang Tract was a particular example. But it was a matter she was not really prepared to debate. China's basic approach was that, while not accepting the McMahon line, she would abide by the alignment until the disputed areas had been sorted out through negotiation. In other words the *status quo* in both East and West should operate until China and India, as equals, reached an agreement and signed a treaty.

In this situation, with China developing territory westward to which India had a good claim and India doing likewise eastward where China had a case for ownership, there was clearly room for negotiation. And since the Aksai Chin was of no earthly use to India, whereas China had little or no interest in NEFA, the problem was by no means intractable. One would have thought that old friends could have got down to some bargaining and adopted a commonsense approach. Certainly for these two great Asian nations to go to war over a bleak wasteland and a few cheerless mountain ridges was unthinkable. As Peking put it in a note to New Delhi in 1959, 'It is impossible to entertain the absurd idea that our two great friendly nations with a combined population of one thousand million should start a war over such temporary and local disputes.' But the days of sweet reasonableness were running out. The 'temporary and local disputes' did start a war – three years later.

In the notes which passed between New Delhi and Peking in the late 'fifties, the Chinese replies to the increasingly belligerent Indian dispatches sound a note of growing incredulity. It is as if the Peking authorities were in a quandary as to how to deal with the Indian Prime Minister, Jawaharlal Nehru, a respected and senior world statesman, a man who held friendship with China as a central plank of his foreign policy and yet was suddenly behaving like a spoiled adolescent leader of some banana republic. They had cause to wonder, and could hardly be blamed if they could find no rational explanation of Nehru's unpredictable behaviour on a question which was admittedly important to both sides but not so important as to obscure other vital matters of mutual interest.

The truth of the matter was that Nehru had got himself into a fix, and he was jumping from the extremes of high-mindedness and moral rectitude to chauvinism and expediency. To go back a little in time, China's move into Tibet in 1950 had alarmed some sections of Indian public opinion and they were keeping a nervous watch on the Himalayas. Their worst fears seemed justified when the discovery of the Aksai Chin road was made known and the Chinese reacted heavily to the 1959 Tibetan revolt. To many in India it seemed that China was becoming something of a 'Big Brother' menace. On the other hand, the Chinese, while admitting New Delhi's right to offer political asylum to the Dalai Lama, were greatly annoyed at what they believed to be Indian interference in Tibetan (and therefore their own) affairs by not only giving sanctuary to Tibetan rebels but actively aiding subversive elements.

From 1959 onwards a new toughness marked India's relations with China. India adopted a more forward policy towards its disputed borders and there was the occasional clash as patrol met patrol. So far as India was concerned, the borders began to assume a wholly disproportionate importance among her national interests. The nation at large, partly through Nehru's ambivalence, was misled into believing that China was somehow 'getting away with it', encroaching upon Indian territory while the Government was trying to be patient and restrained. Public opinion became inflamed and the demands on Nehru for positive action became louder and more strident.

Nehru himself now began to give more refined expression to the spirit of jingoism which was spreading over India like water from a burst dam. The situation obtaining in 1962 was ironic by any standards. Nehru himself had generated the mood which resulted in a more aggressive, hard-headed and stubborn attitude towards China; he had forced the pace of the border dispute, then limited the field for negotiating manoeuvre and one by one closed off all the avenues leading to compromise. Yet he and his colleagues had managed at the same time to convince the electorate that it was China who was squeezing the pressure points to their pride and patience. The inevitable outcome of this double standard of behaviour was that an uninformed public, the Opposition and to some extent the Government demanded some form of action against China. Nehru, who had triggered the jingoism, was backed into a corner where he had to espouse it to save himself. He and his colleagues, Krishna Menon in particular, became guilty of the very sins which they had never refrained from condemning in other national leaders.

It was difficult then and it is difficult still to believe that Nehru could be guilty of such shabbiness. After all, he was the disciple of non-alignment, and had made India the unquestioned spokesman of the Third World. India under his guidance had become the natural leader of all developing nations; she was the respected home of non-violent protest; once the biggest colony of all, she had led the march to freedom. True, she lectured a little overmuch and was quick to find fault in others, but none could question her right to speak on behalf of all former colonies. She was the voice of pacifist, peace-loving nations everywhere. Where there were peace talks or talks of peace India's presence was regarded as mandatory. Even in the Korean War her contribution to the United Nations forces had been a medical unit – and a very respected one at that.

It is understandable, therefore, that the world, looking on at the developing crisis between China and India, assumed that the latter with such a proud and distinguished record in the search for a more peaceful international scene could not possibly be involved in pushing a dispute over borders to a dangerous and absurd point. And yet it was in just such an exercise that India was occupied. She was indulging in a gigantic game of bluff which involved accusing China of the very practices of which she herself was guilty; at one and the same time she was flexing her muscles and engaging in a bout of pacifist breast-beating – a not uncommon performance among New Delhi politicians. It is sometimes overlooked that while India was the home of Gandhi and the birthplace of non-violent protest it is also the home of some of the most martial races under the sun. India's split personality on matters of war and peace, her tendency to arrogant self-deception, was never more aptly illustrated than in the China crisis.

Although by 1962 the relationship between Peking and New Delhi had reached an all-time low, there was still no reason to suppose that the countries would go to war. It was an unhealthy, but far from critical situation. India's temperature, however, continued to rise. Nehru's Government, the source of the infection, had educated the public to believe that although China was encroaching upon the sacred soil of India, the Indian Army was well capable of handling the Chinese should it be called upon to do so. If this was so, the public then asked, why wasn't the Army doing something about it? The question was put with increasing impatience. Nehru now found that he had shadow-boxed himself into a corner, and the only way out was through real action, through some positive move. He had to turn to the Army.

In the first six months of 1962 Indian patrols set up some twenty-four posts along the McMahon Line. The Chinese watched but did not interfere. The *casus belli* was the establishment of a post to the north and beyond the McMahon Line at Dhola. On the Chinese side of the Line was a high crest known as the Thag La Ridge and with the general forward movement in this sector the Ridge became more and more accepted as the Indian frontier although it was obviously beyond it if the McMahon Line on the maps was applied to the ground. Dhola Post was set up beneath the Ridge. The Indians found a sign there proclaiming the area to be Chinese territory, but the Chinese did not react immediately. Some weeks went by before the Chinese approached the post and began to invest it.

All might have remained well if matters had rested there. But now that Thag La Ridge had been accepted in the Indian Government's mind as India's true border, the idea took hold and grew that the Chinese should be evicted from it. The Army was given the job of pushing the Chinese back, and in piecemeal, haphazard fashion battalions of infantry were ordered up to the NEFA region.

The Indians had embarked on a policy of military madness and it was to bring inevitable disaster to their arms. To begin with, the Army commanders had insufficient men to mount the type of operation needed to get the Chinese off the Ridge. Even as it was, the supply and reinforcement of the troops in the area was in itself a major task. It was all but impossible to get supplies up to the men by the overland routes. Some of the forward units were operating at heights of around 15,000–16,000 feet; the terrain was extremely rugged, the atmosphere was rarefied. Physical exertion quickly drained the strength of the soldiers, and many suffered from respiratory trouble. Only air drops could supply them with the required quantities of food, weapons and ammunition, but in that mountainous country dropping sites were difficult to find.

On the Ridge the PLA soldiers watched the increased Indian activity with amused tolerance. They were securely dug in, acclimatized through years of soldiering in Tibet and similar areas. They were well and relatively easily supplied by a network of roads behind their lines. Unlike most of the Indians, they were clothed in warm, padded uniforms. As the demeanour of the Indians became more aggressive, they too began to receive reinforcements.

The Indian commanders in NEFA were appalled at the task the politicians had forced upon them. They protested strongly, pointing out the logistical and manpower problems and the advantageous position in which the Chinese were placed to resist any offensive. A command shake-up was New Delhi's answer to this internal problem. Common sense and realism thus made their exit. The man sent in to assume command of 'Operation Leghorn', the code-name of the Chinese eviction plan, was General B. M. Kaul, who up to 1962 had enjoyed a glittering career but was without front-line experience. He was a charming, cultured and persuasive officer, and he realized that his steady promotions were a source of resentment among some senior officers. He saw in Operation Leghorn an opportunity to silence the critics who

99

yapped behind his back. Anything but success was unthinkable. The deadline for the offensive against the Chinese had been fixed for 10 October, and Kaul decided to keep to the timetable. But of course he faced the same problems as the more outspoken officers who had preceded him. The men were without adequate clothing, they were existing on basic, hard rations and they had little more ammunition than what they could get into their pouches. Yet they were expected to assault well-prepared positions, adequately supported by artillery. Even if the jawans (Indian soldiers) drove off the Chinese, there was little possibility of their being supplied and properly reinforced to fight off the inevitable counter-attack. Yet Kaul pressed on.

Throughout the long period of Indian build-up, the Chinese watched and waited, appraised Indian intentions and prepared for counter-action. Neither Kaul nor anyone else in the High Command gave adequate consideration to how the Chinese would react to a push against Thag La Ridge. So far as this campaign was concerned, Military Intelligence was a contradiction in terms. There seems to have been some vague idea that the Chinese would simply fall back and acquiesce in the occupation of the Ridge. Their previous impassiveness seems to have lulled the Indian High Command into a belief that they would not contest the day, that somehow the Chinese would play along and allow the Indian Army to extricate itself from a totally impossible military situation.

But on 10 October the PLA was in an unforgiving mood. The Chinese had not only worked out their counter-move to any Indian push at Thag La; they knew the day and time it would be launched. Chinese local intelligence was far better than Indian, though it was also considerably helped by the almost total lack of security in New Delhi. Dawn of the 10th found the Indians struggling forward to the dreaded Ridge, some Rajput riflemen out in front. The Chinese reacted viciously. A heavy mortar barrage preceded a general swoop down the slopes. From bunkers and trenches scores of Chinese emerged and bounded down the slopes. They outnumbered the Indians by at least twenty to one. There was no contest. When Kaul saw what was happening he turned to Brigadier Dalvi and gave voice to an expression which was to dog him ever afterwards: 'Oh my God, you're right. They mean business.'

In these spontaneous words Kaul laid bare the whole sham of the Indian political and military forward movement. The day of reckoning had arrived: within a matter of minutes the Indian units were cut to shreds in a hail of mortar bombs, machine-gun bullets and rifle fire. The courage of the jawans could not compensate for the lack of it among those urging them on. They were hurled back in disarray. General Kaul handed over control of the battle to Brigadier Dalvi, a man who was later captured but by his ability and bearing enhanced an already fine reputation; he himself departed for New Delhi to inform his friend the Prime Minister of the new state of affairs.

While he was on his way to attend to his political lines of communication, the PLA disengaged. Two days later he signalled from the capital that the troops were to stay in their positions: no withdrawal. The next day another signal arrived: the objective remained the same; the Chinese must be cleared from the Thag La Ridge.

The Chinese had gone back to their bunkers. They had administered a sharp slap and waited not only on events but upon political instructions from Peking. They had waited and prepared for the Indian attack, such as it was, and had knocked it out within minutes of the jawans leaving their start-lines. But what to do next? From the behaviour and dispositions of the Indians it was clear that they had no intention of withdrawing beyond the McMahon Line; rather, it seemed, they were preparing to have another go. The reverse they had suffered appeared to be having no effect on their purpose. In actual fact the Indians, men and officers alike, were appalled at the situation in which they found themselves, but they had to do what they were told, and Kaul was telling them to stay where they were.

The High Command in Peking had a tricky problem. Was the negative policy of simply holding the line at Thag La and allowing the Indians to stay in advance of the *status quo* line, any longer worth while? The world already believed that India was the victim of aggression. Was anything to be gained by the Chinese maintaining their present policy? Obviously not. India was certainly winning the propaganda war, even though making a fool of herself in military terms. But few people knew what was really happening in NEFA. Some time after 10 October Mao and the High Command of the PLA decided that the long-term advantages of counter-action were worth the risk of the additional opprobium which would be heaped upon her. From a military point of view everything was in China's favour. Their intelligence sources told them of the ridiculous muddle into which the Indians had got themselves, and observation of Indian positions and deployment revealed that there was little to stop a determined attack. The Chinese had the advantage in numbers, heavy weapons and supply routes; they also had the initiative. There were other factors for Peking to consider. Winter was approaching and if an attack was to be launched and a victory secured there was little time available before the snows restricted troop movements. The offensive would have to be on such a scale and of such an intensity that Indian resistance would be overwhelmed within a matter of weeks. Such a shattering blow might result in the Indian leaders being brought to their senses and back to the negotiating table.

To sit on Thag La Ridge throughout the winter or indefinitely after that did not make military sense. In time the initiative might pass to the Indian Army, and the PLA would be able to react only at the time and place chosen by India. Such a prolonged confrontation would place a severe strain on the PLA's logistical problems. To go over to the attack involved few military risks, though the political risks were many.

Indian and Western commentators have suggested that the Chinese offensive had other objectives besides those of occupying territories she claimed as her own. These are said to have included the shaking of the faith of the Indian peoples in Nehru's government, the subversion of the five-year economic plan by forcing a transfer of resources, and the demonstration to the rest of the world, but to the Communist nations in particular, that China was the natural leader of the Asian peoples; since India and Russia were drawing closer, any war would force Moscow to choose sides. If she chose India then her unreliability as an ally would be revealed to other Communist nations. If these objectives were considered at all in Peking, then very likely they were secondary to the more pressing military aims and problems. Some of these political repercussions followed the successful conclusion of the campaign, but they came as a result of the war rather than being objectives of it. For it must be remembered that India hastened the pace of the quarrel and brought on the conflict. If China had nursed these ulterior motives she would surely have started the provocation in order to bring on a general engagement.

China's war aims were simpler than have been made out. She decided to administer a sharp drubbing to India in order to stop her attempts to alter the border by unilateral action. Her withdrawal from occupied territory after the ceasefire emphasized that she was not looking for additional territory but for a settled and regulated border. Nor was she seeking to impose a settlement. The objective was to take the tension out of the border situation, deflate India's swelling ardour for military conclusions and, if possible, get her to respond to a suggestion of new border talks. As Neville Maxwell puts it,* 'China had been engaged not on an invasion of India, but on a giant punitive expedition', and there was general surprise at her action only because the Indian version of what was happening in NEFA had been widely accepted as the correct one.

After the abortive Indian foray on Thag La on 10 October, China began to order up additional PLA units from Tibet until she had an estimated three divisions in the NEFA area. She made no secret of her preparations. This time the Indians waited, watched and worried.

Shortly after five o'clock on the morning of 20 October two signal flares arched into the air above the Chinese lines. The cascade of light brought forth a blistering barrage of artillery and mortar shells on the Indian positions across the Namka Chu river line below Thag La. The Red soldiers came down the Ridge behind the lifting barrage and swept away the jawans in front of them.

* *India's China War*, p. 414.

The Chinese Red Army

They came on in overwhelming numbers, but immediately probed for the flanks of positions whence Indian small-arms fire was heavy and concentrated. The Gorkhalis and Rajputs fought stubbornly, often to the last round and the last man, but they never had a chance. Their positions were widely separated and the jawans were unable to give each other supporting or covering fire. The PLA men infiltrated and isolated each pocket of resistance and then rushed in to swamp it. By nine o'clock it was all over. The Namka Chu line, which was never more than a political gesture, was finished. The Indians in the rifle pits had fought longer and better than the politicians in New Delhi had the right to expect.

Much the same was happening thousands of miles away in the Western or Ladakh sector. Here the Red Army used similar tactics to those in NEFA – a preliminary bombardment quickly followed up by racing infantry. And again the luckless Indians who had been thrust forward in isolated posts soon found themselves cut off. Pathetic radio signals were the last testaments of many of these forsaken units. There was nothing anyone could do for them. They either died where they stood or surrendered.

The Chinese had opened up a two-front war, but the main weight of the offensive was in NEFA where a three-pronged attack down from Thag La had the Indians reeling in confusion. At every point of anticipated strong resistance the Chinese applied superior forces of men and guns. But characteristically the Red soldiers, confident of success, tended to expose themselves and exhibit that over-confidence which leads to unnecessary casualties. Where the Indians fought it out with matchless and thankless courage, they took a heavy toll. And the Chinese quickly appreciated that they were not involved in a total walk-over and became just that little bit more circumspect.

With the débâcle at Thag La Indian attention focused on a fall-back position at Se La, a 14,600-feet-high pass which from the maps and a cursory glance at the terrain seemed to offer an impregnable defensive position. Se La offered distinct advantages, it is true. With the enemy coming straight down the road from Thag La, his passage could be interdicted. Frontal assaults could be broken up before ever they got going, and after the initial holding

104

action the position could be reinforced and built up so as to be unassailable. But there were disadvantages. Because of its height and the difficult country around it the supply and reinforcement problems would remain much the same as they were further forward, and the soldiers would experience just the same physical problems as they had contesting high-altitude ground at Thag La. There were arguments but eventually Se La was decided upon. And the jawans pulling back or wandering back from Thag La and the Tawang Tract gathered at the pass.

The Chinese knew all about Se La and appreciated that it was a formidable obstacle if properly and adequately defended. Logically, therefore, they probed and patrolled with their accustomed speed and efficiency for the flank or weak spot. (It should be noted at this point that the PLA could have obviated many of its difficulties by thrusting at the same time through the border kingdom of Bhutan. For obvious political reasons she chose not to do so. Many Indian stragglers escaped the Chinese net, however, by routing themselves either by accident or design through neutral Bhutan.)

With the hasty reorganization of the Indian defences and the methodical Chinese occupation of Tawang and approach to Se La, a brief phoney war developed. A wave of patriotic fervour swept India from Kashmir to Kerala; the nation was said to be united as never before; a backs-to-the-wall spirit of Dunkirk was evinced; Nehru's vacillations were reported to have Churchillian tones. Pacifist India found that nothing concentrated the mind quite so wonderfully as war, albeit undeclared.

American, British and French aircraft flew in massive quantities of arms in response to India's pleas for help. The Third World, the non-aligned nations unable to help materially, also failed to give India moral support, and this was a wound as deep as any China could inflict. As if by some sixth sense India's pacifist or neutralist friends had divined what was going on and the political consequences. They drew back.

The phoney war also gave India an opportunity to indulge in the national pastime of self-deception. The Army was said to be preparing to throw back the invader; confidence and morale were never higher. The jawans were just waiting for an opportunity to get to grips with the Chinese whose encroachment had reached its limit. The days of counter-attack and victory were at hand.

In contrast the war was very much played down in China. The press and radio concentrated on the political aspects of the tussle and there was no attempt to stimulate a war frenzy in the nation. Chou En-lai allowed himself a few exaggerations as to the scale of the Indian attack at Thag La, but by and large the Chinese were moderate in their propaganda and played out the tragedy with an eye to winning as quickly as possible and not making a permanent, unforgiving enemy of India. The political calculation was done to a nicety.

On the approaches to Se La, however, the PLA was rather more direct. Engineers were busy blasting a road through from the McMahon Line to Se La. The Chinese commanders were not taking any chances about supply routes, and for the Indians the implication was obvious. Once the road was through and trucks were moving, the attacks would be renewed. PLA patrols and scouting parties were out day and night and by the time the road was usable their work too would be done. The Indians continued their build up at Se La and behind and down the line at Dirang Dzong and Bomdi La. But they employed nothing like the concentrated application of the Chinese to overcome their organizational and supply problems. Command changes once again upset the Indians. General Kaul, who had been ill, returned to the front to retrieve the Army's and his own reputation after the Thag La setback.

Over in the Eastern sector of NEFA the Indians tried a sortie against the Chinese at Walong on 14 November – Nehru's birthday. A success on such an auspicious day was reckoned as being an ideal morale-booster for Army, Government and the public. The 6th Kumaonis were given the task of throwing the Chinese off a dominating hill feature. Tired but not dispirited after days of patrolling, the Kumaonis, who are not unlike the Gorkhalis in that they are hill folk, stocky and sturdy in appearance, went up the hillside in fine style, only to be cut down by machine guns from well-concealed bunkers. The attack was uncoordinated and not properly supported. Once again the Chinese were allowed to win a victory because of a gesture against them rather than a properly planned military operation. The PLA men seized the initiative and counter-attacked strongly. The Indians broke under the pressure and 11 Brigade, like its companion the 7th on the Namka Chu, disintegrated.

Meanwhile in the Se La/Bomdi La sector the Chinese had blown their road through to Tawang and were busily improving the existing road up to Se La. The Indians had 62 Brigade at Se La, 48 Brigade at Bomdi La and midway between the two 65 Brigade and divisional headquarters at Dirang Dzong. Each position, one behind the other, offered good defensive fields of fire. But the key to the unlocking of the whole vertical chain of widely separated posts simply had to be placed in a side door. Such a door was provided by the Bailey Trail, a route named after a British explorer, which came through the mountains on the Indian right and would bring anyone coming up it behind the Dirang Dzong position and in front of Bomdi La. With the road cut, Se La/Dirang Dzong would be isolated and finished. Late on in the day the Indians became concerned about the Trail. It was too late. PLA units had already found it and were moving along in some strength. The Indian 5th Guards were sent to block the route, but on 17 November some 1500 Chinese hurled themselves against the Guards. It was a tough battle, but the day went to the Chinese because, as was now becoming a common feature in this campaign, the Indians were given a job to do and then left unsupported. The Red soldiers kept up the pressure on the Guards until the latter, having run out of ammunition, were given the order to withdraw. In their attempt to disengage, the Indians forfeited all cohesion. Survivors of the action lost themselves in the surrounding jungle country. The 5th Guards ceased to exist and the Red soldiers raced forward to cut the vital Se La/Bomdi La road. Se La and Dirang Dzong had become untenable. The Chinese appreciated this more quickly than the Indians. Meanwhile the PLA regiments in front of Se La put in a probing, exploratory attack and suffered considerable casualties in the exercise. The 4th Garhwal Rifles threw back the first attack and resisted four more as the

107

Chinese tried to press forward and turn the scales of an action which was going against them.

The Indian commander at Se La now began to fear for his rear. Chinese patrols were all about, cutting roads and tracks and ambushing straying parties. He asked for permission to fall back on Bomdi La while he still had a chance of extricating his command. Indecisiveness and confusion over what to do at Se La gave the position and ultimate victory to the Chinese. And the way was opened for the PLA with a minimum of fighting. As forward units probed the Indian positions they caught an Indian battalion withdrawing. The Red soldiers quickly occupied the vacated positions and opened fire on neighbouring Indian units. The jawans, already shaken and baffled by the unexplained withdrawal of their companions, broke under this sudden hail of fire from an unexpected quarter. The Brigade commander then gave the order for the pull out. For the Chinese, Se La was an easy victory. The pass would have inevitably fallen to them, but they could count themselves fortunate that they did not have to pay the full terms the Indians could have extracted.

Now the Chinese were in full swing. Down the line at Dirang Dzong they brought the Indian divisional headquarters under fire. Infiltration again paid its dividends in Indian panic and fever to get back to safety. As the units pulled out they were ambushed. Many were killed, more were captured and a few escaped to the plains below.

There now remained Bomdi La. Here lay 48 Brigade. It was much denuded of men but still reasonably strong and supported by artillery, mortars and four light tanks. The Chinese were in too great a strength for any hope to be held out for a prolonged defence, but nevertheless the Indians were well entrenched and in a mood to demand a high price for the surrender of the position. But once again Indian leadership exerted itself to assist the Chinese. General Kaul rang through to Brigadier Gurbax Singh and ordered him to send a mobile column up to Dirang Dzong. Neither the Brigade commander nor Kaul were aware that Dirang Dzong had already fallen, but Gurbax Singh protested the order. He pointed out that his promised reinforcements had not arrived and that if he reduced his command further Bomdi La would be impossible to hold against a concerted attack. Kaul brushed aside the protest and Gurbax Singh ordered the column to be formed up. It consisted of two infantry companies, two light tanks and two mountain guns. Hardly had it left the vicinity of Bomdi La than the Chinese assault erupted all around.

The Indians resisted stoutly, but the Chinese, who had spotted the movement forward of the column, immediately probed for positions vacated by these troops. In their usual, professional manner they quickly located the weak spots and systematically began to infiltrate the Brigade. Meanwhile the column commander on his way to a lost cause heard the opening shots of one behind him. He ordered the column back down the road and drove straight into a carefully prepared ambush. The Indians were decimated. The battle for Bomdi La had now become fierce. The Chinese hurled themselves at the Indian positions. There was much hand-to-hand fighting, bayonet screeching against bayonet, and the Indian gunners fired over open sights in desperate efforts to stem the increasing tide of Red soldiers washing up in front of them.

It was heroic but useless. By late afternoon Brigade headquarters was under small-arms fire. The defence of Bomdi La was long past the hopeless stage, and Gurbax Singh gave the word to fall back down the road to Rupa where defensive positions had been prepared. No sooner had the remnants of the Brigade arrived in Rupa than General Kaul ordered them to keep going on to Chaku. So on they went with the PLA light troops hard on their heels. Kaul now intervened again. He changed his mind and ordered the Brigade back to Rupa. But it was too late. The Chinese gunners were already spraying it with artillery and mortar shells. A now thoroughly demoralized 48 Brigade retraced its steps back to Chaku. Again it was too late. The Chinese had the place surrounded. They ambushed a column taking up supplies and ammunition and then, after plastering the area with a vicious barrage, stormed in and scattered the defenders like so much chaff in the wind. As suddenly as it had begun it was all over. With Chaku in their hands and the Indian defence force in NEFA smashed into pieces, the way into the plains of Assam lay open. There was no organized Indian force available to offer any resistance. In nineteen days the PLA had obliterated the equivalent of three Indian infantry divisions (they did not, of course, fight as such but in scattered, hastily gathered formations of varying sizes and descriptions). All the Chinese had claimed was now within their grasp – and more was available for the taking. Two days later they announced that they intended to give it all up and would return to the previous line of control.

Over in the Western sector the Indians avoided a débâcle on the scale of the NEFA action. There were good reasons for this. Chinese objectives were more limited, and in a sense they were fighting a holding action – much as India was to do a decade later in the war against Pakistan when a revitalized Army held the Western sector in a deadlock while invading East Pakistan and assisting the foundation of Bangladesh. Once the Chinese reached their claim line in Ladakh they stopped. The Indian Command in this sector did not make sacrificial gestures. Ground was only held when it was considered vital in the buying of time, and the Indians steadily built up their reserves and prepared for a long war, eschewing the temptations to make headlines in Calcutta, Bombay and New Delhi, through the useless throwing away of the lives of the jawans which would have been reported in heroic but fatuous terms. The war ended here at the same time as it did in NEFA.

For the Chinese it was a spectacular victory brought about by their own strict observance of the rules of warfare and hastened by the Indian disregard for them. Few soldiers have been asked to endure what the jawans were called upon to endure, and they brought no discredit upon themselves. The Chinese respected their fighting qualities; indeed, Chinese casualties were probably as heavy as those suffered by the Indians. Three years elapsed before the Indian Defence Ministry released its figures. It was then reported that 1383 jawans had been killed in action, 1696 were missing and 3968 had been taken prisoner. The Chinese repatriated the sick and wounded very quickly, and the majority of prisoners were returned within weeks of the ceasefire.

It is no part of this story to go into the ceasefire proposals and

110

subsequent arguments. Suffice it to say that China succeeded in taking the heat out of the border situation, but failed in the longer-term objective of bringing the dispute to the negotiating table. An armed truce still operates on the borders. India has embraced the Soviet Union even more closely, confirming China's suspicions, and still maintains that she was the aggrieved party, the victim of unprovoked aggression. But her position of speaker-in-chief for the non-aligned nations has been considerably undermined.

China's exercise of her military power impressed her Asian neighbours, and the unilateral withdrawal impressed them and other nations even more. It seems unlikely that she will come to blows with India again. She has confirmed her hold on the Aksai Chin and does not appear too bothered about the NEFA claim. In time the two nations will probably settle their differences amicably. It all depends on how soon the Indians can bring themselves to admit that in 1962 they may not have been altogether in the right. It will be a bitter pill to swallow, and one which the Indian political digestive system is certainly not capable of absorbing at the moment.

CONFRONTATION WITH RUSSIA: 1969-1973

The Chinese Government has never hidden the
fact that there exist irreconcilable
differences of principle between China and
the Soviet Union and that the struggle of
principle between them will continue for a
long period of time. . . . There is no reason
whatsoever for China and the Soviet Union
to go to war over the boundary question –
Peking policy statement

The Russians said it was deliberate murder. And of course
Moscow's version of the deadly clash between Soviet and Chinese
border guards along the Ussuri River on 2 March 1969 supports
the statement. A whole section of Russian guards died under the
hail of bullets suddenly let loose by the Chinese. The Peking
leaders, while stoutly denying the accusation of 'murder', have not
released their evidence of events. They rarely do. The Russians
also are usually secretive about what happens on their sensitive
frontiers, but after the incident of 2 March they took the unusual
step of informing the world in considerable detail about the fighting which flared up so dramatically on Damansky Island (or Chen
Pao Island, as it is known to the Chinese).

The island lies in the wide Ussuri about 100 miles south of
Khabarovsk and some 250 miles north of Vladivostok, Russia's
vital port outlet into the eastern waters, which is situated on the
edge of a tongue of land slipping down the north-eastern side of
China.

A sparsely populated area, the lands around the Ussuri at this
point are thickly forested and there is rumoured to be great
mineral wealth beneath. Through this undulating country runs the
Trans-Siberian Railway linking the European and Asian halves of
Russia. At one point the line meanders to within three miles of the
border, becoming vulnerable to a Chinese thrust. Indeed, any

forward movement by the Chinese would not only cut this vital artery but slice off the peninsula on which Vladivostok is placed. Thus at one stroke China could deny Russia both access to its gigantic naval base and entry into Eastern and Pacific waters. Hence any Chinese agitation on the Ussuri strikes panic in the Kremlin.

Moscow's feverish denunciation of Chinese 'aggression' on 2 March initially caused the West some amusement. After all, here not only were the two biggest Communist nations falling out in public, but their border guards were killing each other. But as incident followed incident, with mounting casualties on both sides, and as the two giants squared up to each other, amusement turned to alarm, for this was clearly no mere extension of the ideological quarrel exacerbated by a few hotheads with jumpy trigger fingers but a serious confrontation which could precipitate the participants into war – a war which would inevitably become nuclear and involve the whole world.

The world was on the brink of a crisis and the focal point was an unknown island in an unknown river in an unknown part of Asia. And what was happening there no one really knew, since there were only the selective statements from Moscow and Peking on which to base a judgment. All that was certain was that the Soviet Union and China were escalating a long-standing dispute not just over one river island but over hundreds of miles of their common border and that the immediate argument over whether the Ussuri border ran along the centre of the river (normal international practice) as the Chinese claimed, or along the Chinese river bank as the Russians said, served only as an inadequate mask over deeper, more significant and dangerous differences between them. (A centre of river border would give the advantage to the Chinese should they want seriously to disrupt Russian river traffic since the deep channels would come under their control.) The flashpoint was Damansky/Chen Pao Island. Was it to become the Sarajevo of 1969?

To look into what happened on that fateful, bitterly cold morning of 2 March we have to rely on Russian sources. One of the fuller descriptions of the shooting incident has been supplied by

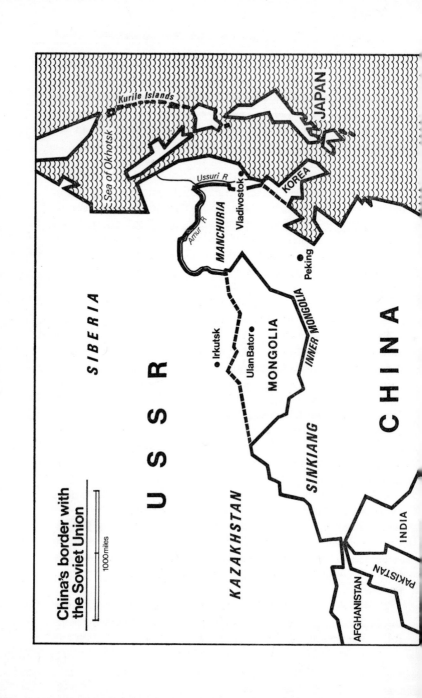

China's border with
the Soviet Union

1000miles

S I B E R I A

U S S R

KAZAKHSTAN

Irkutsk

UlanBator

MONGOLIA

SINKIANG

INNER MONGOLIA

C H I N A

AFGHANISTAN

PAKISTAN

INDIA

Sea of Okhotsk

Kurile Islands

Ussuri R

Amur R

MANCHURIA

Vladivostok

KOREA

Peking

JAPAN

two Army journalists, Lieut.-Col. V. Nagorny and Lieut.-Col. B. Prichkin, who were sent to cover the 'war front'. Their report of the clash was issued later in March through Soviet embassy information channels. It is larded with the usual amount of hyperbole and patriotic exhortation, but, pruned of inessentials, the story, though second-hand, is interesting. It has the ring of truth, but the vital passage dealing with the Chinese shooting, the evidence of 'murder', is open to various interpretation and will be looked at later.

According to these two reporters, a Soviet observation post near Damansky Island reported to headquarters on the morning of 2 March that a group of armed Chinese frontier guards were moving out of their own post at Gun Hsi and heading towards the southern tip of the island, a move made possible by the solid freezing of the Ussuri. Senior Lieutenant I. Strelnikov, who was in command of that section of the frontier, gathered an armed party of his own and set out across the snow and ice to intercept the intruders. The Russians, said the writers, wore their weapons across their chests. The Chinese guards were in two groups, one of eighteen men and the other of twelve. Strelnikov stepped forward in front of his men and accused the Chinese of violating the Russian border.

Of what happened next, the two men wrote: 'The officer was not able to finish his angry protest. The first row of violators, who had unquestionably rehearsed their actions beforehand, at once stood aside to enable the provokers behind them to fire point-blank at our border guards.

'Artillery and mortars opened fire from the Chinese shore. As we learned later, the Chinese had long prepared for this bandit raid. In addition to the armed detachment that they sent to the island, they deployed large units of a total strength of some 300 men in the snow and on the flanks. Positions for mortars and anti-tank guns, stationed for direct fire, were arranged beforehand and thoroughly camouflaged.

'Though the Soviet border guards had lost their commanding officer and the men with him, they did not flinch but engaged in unequal combat. Command was taken by Junior Sergeant Yuri

Babanski, a platoon commander, who deployed his small group of men in the natural folds of the island. Under his command the soldiers put up a gallant stand until reinforcements arrived.'

The reinforcements were led by Senior Lieutenant V. Bubenin in an armoured personnel carrier. He attempted to cut off the retreat of the more exposed Chinese, but his carrier was knocked out by an anti-tank gun. Private P. Kovalyov, the carrier driver, rescued the lieutenant and other wounded men from the burning wreck. Local volunteers now arrived on the scene with a sleigh which they used for taking back the wounded men and ferrying ammunition up to the guards who were down to their last few rounds.

Lidia Strelnikov, the widow of the frontier guard officer, went to the border post on hearing the firing and helped the doctor to tend the injured 'with no thought for herself'. Mrs. Strelnikov was without doubt a very courageous woman on that day.

When the Chinese pulled back to their line and the firing died away, the Russians found they had 31 dead and 14 wounded. These were the figures given by the Tass news agency. The Chinese suffered losses but the numbers are not known.

The question posed after the brief but savage action was whether the first Russian deaths were the result of a carefully planned provocation, its intention being the cold-blooded shooting down of a group of unsuspecting border guards. The leaders in the Kremlin believed this to be so; at least they said so. Or were their shrill protests, so dramatically relayed to the world, a cover for their own aggression along the border? If on 2 March the Russians were not actually sinners, neither were they saints. A review of the situation that day along the frozen wastes of the Ussuri indicates that all the blame does not necessarily lie on Chinese shoulders.

For months past, tension along the whole 4500-mile Sino-Soviet border, the longest between any two countries in the world, had been building up as the Moscow–Peking split widened and both sides adopted a hard-headed no-surrender attitude on territorial matters. The situation along the Ussuri River and its tributary, the Amur, had been particularly strained and fraught with dangers, but still frontier units maintained communications with their opposite numbers so that there was at least some understanding of each other's role, attitudes and likely intentions. Also, both Russian and Chinese unit commanders must have had weighty standing orders covering every likely eventuality.

When Lieut. Strelnikov went out to meet the advancing Chinese, it is probable that he expected another arguing match, perhaps a little pushing and shoving, a common occurrence at that time, and then a return to their original positions, with honour satisfied on both sides. The Army journalists say the guards had their weapons across their chests and there is no cause to doubt the truth of this statement. What they do not relate is the manner in which the Chinese carried their own arms. If they advanced in a threatening manner then Strelnikov was foolhardy, to say the least, in leading his men out on to the ice with their arms secured in the safe position. But perhaps the Chinese had also their weapons slung.

There is no arguing with the fact that the Chinese intrusion on the island was deliberate and, in the light of the political situation, provocative. But it has been a practice of the Chinese to establish a physical presence, wherever possible, on territory they claim for their own. Sometimes they attempt to make a permanent post, sometimes they let it be known they have 'staked their claim' and then retire. The expedition to Damansky Island was of the latter type.

The Russian report says the Chinese had mortars and anti-tank guns sited on the island and camouflaged. This lends credence to the ambush theory. But since the Ussuri border area was and still is under contention, of course the Chinese had guns in position. So had the Russians. Both river banks were armed camps. The point is that when the Chinese patrol went forward the men were expecting trouble and consequently nervous of what might happen. The men at the mortars and anti-tank guns were ready to support them and give them covering fire should anything go wrong. Trouble and tension nipped the air as much as the frost. Perhaps the Chinese were too ready in their anticipation of aggressive Russian reaction, over-prepared to reach for their weapon triggers.

It is stressed by the Russians that before Strelnikov could

finish his verbal protest the front row of Chinese fell back, allow-ing those behind to fire into the Soviet guards from a few feet away. But was this action really so deliberate, quite so rehearsed? It must be remembered that these men had been eyeing one another for months on end, glaring at one another across the frozen wastes. Tempers and nerves were strained, Chinese passions running high after a long period of concentrated and excited anti-Russian propaganda. The guards were like so many leashed gladiators prowling the arena.

During the confrontation on the island it is well within the bounds of possibility that either Strelnikov or one of his men made a threatening gesture or a sudden movement which was im-mediately interpreted by the Chinese as a signal to the Russian lines for fire to be brought down on them. Strelnikov was almost certainly shouting in Russian and it is doubtful if the Chinese understood what he was saying. Ready to think the worst, already highly nervous and prepared to jump to conclusions, they opened fire.

The Soviet reporters say that the Chinese in front gave way to allow those behind a field of fire. This again is probably quite true. The back-up party may well have had instructions to fire on a given word – and the word could have come on a misinterpretation of what the Russians intended to do.

There is another possibility. The Soviet guards may themselves have misread Chinese intentions and attempted to go for their own guns.

Although this is all conjecture, almost certainly something of this sort happened. A terrible error of judgment brought on by men having been made to endure an intolerable level of strain over a long period is a more plausible explanation than that of a deli-berately planned murder, as the Russians maintain. The Chinese 'defence' is also strengthened when one looks at how the patrol found itself on the island. Such a probe forward could only have been ordered at divisional level, and the commander would only have ordered such a move after being given specific instructions from Peking. The decision to demonstrate the claim to Damansky would have had to be made at the very top, by Mao himself. He was the only man who could give the word for an operation so risky and fraught with danger; and it is highly unlikely that either he or anyone below him would authorize the planning of a deliberate murder, the callous shooting down of unsuspecting Russians. The risks of going on to the island could be reasonably calculated; but no one could be sure of the consequences of the killing of a guard unit in quite the manner suggested by Moscow. The result could have been the bringing on of a general engagement, the spread of fighting along the whole border, even nuclear war. Had the Chinese considered such an action, its dangers were so obvious as to make it unacceptable. As it turned out, the Russians limited their retaliation after the 'murders', and this suggests that they too did not completely accept their own theory. After all, the participants on their side, according to the evidence, were all dead. If there were witnesses on the Russian side, and presumably there were, then the Russians were not quite so unprepared as they like to make out.

The suggestion implicit in the Russian version of the Damansky fighting is that the Soviet guards were killed as a result of Chinese deceit and trickery, the sort of thing one would expect of an Oriental. Moscow's propaganda was directed mainly to Westerners and it was presented in such a way as to strike a responsive chord among those prepared to believe in stories of Asian duplicity. That they failed to evoke the expected sympathy was due to a number of considerations and not least to the Chinese handling of their own publicity and propaganda.

After the first Russian denunciation Peking pointed out that in the past ten years there had been thousands of clashes of one sort or another along many stretches of the border and that in some of these incidents there had been casualties. But on these occasions neither side had given them publicity. Why were the Russians making such a big issue out of the Damansky Island fight when there had been similar affairs on the Manchurian, Mongolian and Sinkiang frontiers? This was the question China posed, without eliciting a satisfactory answer, and went on to deflect Moscow's expansionist charges by gleefully exploiting Russia's continuing embarrassment at the recent Czechoslovakia invasion. The Soviet record in eastern Europe, culminating in tanks in the streets of

The Chinese Red Army

Prague and the Cuban missile crisis, did not assist the Russian leaders in their attempt to appear the wronged but patient party. For the first time for many years people around the world were prepared to accept that China might well have a case.

Meanwhile Russia, as usual on these occasions, reserved the right to take whatever steps she felt necessary to stop Chinese provocation and intrusion into her territory, while China responded by announcing that the whole of her frontier with Russia from Central Asia to Manchuria was in dispute.

As the war of words was fought out from the capitals the situation along the Ussuri continued to deterioriate. Along the Ussuri and the Amur, clashes became more frequent, with sometimes substantial casualties on both sides. On at least one occasion the Russians put down quite a heavy artillery bombardment which caught and killed many PLA men in the more forward and exposed riverbank positions. Spring came to these frozen reaches, bringing a thaw which turned large areas near the rivers into marsh and swamp, and both sides had to pull back to previously prepared positions. The thaw ruled out any possibility of an invasion either by the Chinese or the Russians but there was no lessening in the harsh temperatures in which their dispute was trapped. And incidents continued. For instance, in July the Chinese opened fire on Soviet river transport workers near Goldinsky Island. The Russians are said to have gone to the island to repair river navigation markers. If so, they chose an odd time; such a move was bound to irritate the Chinese, who laid claim to the island. One worker was killed and three others wounded by a grenade.

After this attack the Soviet Government announced that it was compelled to take 'additional measures against the actions of the Chinese authorities' in order to protect its 'legitimate rights'. What the additional measures were the Russians did not specify, but they certainly involved the ordering up of more troops into the area. Throughout these tense, charged months there were frequent reports of Russians and Chinese conducting large-scale exercises in the border regions, and both sides heavily reinforced thin border guard divisions with regular army units.

120

Confrontation with Russia: 1969-1973

The border incidents in 1969 were so frequent and selectively reported in their detail by the two governments that it is impossible to apportion blame for the crisis. Both sides were provocative, the Chinese offering the supreme insult by defecating in the Ussuri with their backs to the Russians, and aggressive. In the parallel propaganda battle the opening rounds went to the Russians as they were quickly off the mark to give their version of events. The clash of 2 March was the first to be disclosed, and the earlier detailed review of it shows how difficult it is to assess responsibility for that and a score of similar occurrences. In their counter-attack the Chinese skilfully played their Czechoslovakia card and finessed with the revelation that Russia had asked the Warsaw Pact countries for troops to serve in their eastern regions, and that the Communist bloc countries had not responded to the invitation. But the hands-down triumph for the Chinese came from the way they developed and argued their frontier claims through the propaganda channels. And they had a more receptive audience than in past confrontations.

Peking made great use of the history of the border quarrel from the days of the Tsars, and it is to the period of Russian-Chinese imperial history that one has to look for the sources of the present-day trouble.

The Sino-Soviet border in the East is defined by the Amur River (named by the Chinese the River of the Black Dragon), the Ussuri and the Argun. Russian explorers established trading posts in the Amur region in the 17th century, but were later forced out by the Chinese. The Treaty of Nerchinsk (1689), the first signed by China with a foreign power, settled the border some 700 miles north of where Vladivostok is situated today. For a time Russia calmed her eagerness for eastern expansion but maintained a presence in the region through traders and trappers. Meanwhile the Manchu rulers extended China's domains to include Mongolia and Siankiang while putting a firm clamp on Tibet and the northern Amur area.

The 19th century, however, found China at her weakest. She was unable to resist the invaders from the West, but as she made feeble efforts to do so and her attention was diverted from the

121

north, the Russians, alive again to territorial opportunity, pushed forward and secured the Amur River as their Far Eastern boundary. The Treaty of Aigun in 1858 secured and legalized this frontier. A decadent and distracted Peking Government had given away 190,000 square miles of territory. Two years later Russia used her diplomatic skills to mediate on behalf of the Chinese with her British, French and other European enemies. As a reward for this easy exercise she gained a further 200,000 square miles of Chinese territory to the east of the Ussuri. The Treaty of Peking dignified the robbery.

By the turn of the century Russia had managed to obtain by one means or another some 586,000 square miles of the Middle Kingdom and would probably have gained more but for the war with Japan in 1905. Japan inflicted a crushing defeat on the Russian armies and stopped the eastern expansion. Of perhaps more long-term importance, Japan demonstrated to all Asians that the European could be beaten at his own game of war. This Japanese victory boosted Asian nationalism and signalled the beginning of the end of Western domination of the East. Russians today still smart at this blow to their pride.

After the Communists seized power in Russia Lenin gave a public pledge that the Chinese territory ceded to the Tsars under the unequal treaties would revert 'naturally, automatically and Marxistically' to its 'legitimate Chinese owners'. This promise was never fulfilled, and it will be recalled that after the Goldinsky Island fighting the Kremlin leaders were talking of Russia's 'legitimate rights' over the same territory that Lenin had been prepared to give up. The Chinese now point out that of all the imperial powers who once took land from China only the Russians have failed to hand it back. With a thin smile they point out that the Kremlin leaders are just as empire-minded as their predecessors the Tsars.

The Russians won their territory through the exercise of military might and diplomacy, taking advantage of a sorely tried Manchu dynasty. Moscow's attitude now is that China is attempting to set the clock back, interfere with the 'historical process' and abrogate 'solemn treaties'. The Peking line is that treaties and boundaries should be re-negotiated, that they can only apply if both parties were on an equal footing at the time their signatures were appended. It must be said, however, that the Chinese are not always consistent in their approach, for they are not prepared to discuss areas gained in the days of the Manchu dynasty and since retained. Territories lost in the subsequent decades of weakness are now her bleeding wounds of injured pride. The Chinese position, however, has remained basically the same in her argument with Russia. She holds, with reason, that boundaries should be re-negotiated but accepts that a degree of horse-trading is possible if on both sides there is goodwill and a genuine desire to reach agreement. The Chinese are not asking for everything which was lost to the Tsars to be returned. Clearly this would be un-realistic, and of course totally unacceptable to Russia. China's bargaining position is tough, but it does allow for manoeuvre, some give-and-take.

For the most part, attention during the Sino-Soviet border dispute has centred on the Manchurian–Ussuri–Amur area, but another area of friction has been, and continues to be, the border of Sinkiang, an autonomous region of the People's Republic which houses the Chinese nuclear weapon testing site and her missile galleries.

In this Central Asian area China has an 1800-mile contested frontier which extends from Mongolia to Afghanistan. It is a mountainous region with some peaks rising to 20,000 feet above sea-level. The 1860 Treaty of Peking and the St Petersburg Treaty, signed twenty-one years later, fixed the Sinkiang border with the exception of some 150 miles opposite Afghanistan.

The population on both sides of the Central Asian border is largely Muslim and is made up of a confusing number of tribes, the majority of whom are of the nomadic variety. On the Russian side live Kazakhs and Kirghiz while the Chinese area has some five million Uygurs and large numbers of Kazakhs, Kirghiz and Tajiks. During the days of the Tsars Russia made a determined effort to colonize these wild and untamed zones bringing in non-Muslim peoples from other areas. Russian influence, political, military and economic, was dominant right up to the Second

123

World War. It then went into steep decline, particularly in Sinkiang. After the 1949 take-over in China the Communists made a determined drive to 're-colonize' Sinkiang and intensified their settlement programme after the final liquidation of Soviet influence through the ending of the local joint-stock companies in 1954. These companies had given the Russians an opportunity to maintain at least an economic edge in the area.

In 1945 the Chinese proportion of the total population was estimated at only 3 per cent, but now it is believed to be about 50 per cent. The Chinese colonization programme was given an impetus through the decision to use Sinkiang's vast deserts as a nuclear testing ground, and there was a consequent flow of scientists, technicians and ancillary workers into the area. Chinese-style education, administration and political training were introduced to the local peoples, and attempts were made to settle the nomads. But the nomadic peoples, the majority of whom are linked ethnically and culturally with the inhabitants of Russian Turkestan, objected to the increasing Chinese presence. In 1958 they revolted. There were numerous clashes between the Kazakhs and the Chinese until 1962, when thousands of these nomads and semi-nomads moved over the border into Russia. The Chinese accused Moscow of enticing these people and using them for subversive purposes. Both sides charged each other with violating the frontiers 'thousands of times', charges which mean little when the nature of the country and its inhabitants are taken into consideration.

During the 'sixties the Russians were relatively quiet about the Sinkiang border and made little propaganda from a situation which invited it. They even played down the reported exodus of 60,000 Kazakhs from the Ili district of Sinkiang into their territory. The reason for this unnatural quiet was probably the anxiety of the Soviet military not to draw attention to the build-up of troops and bases. When the Ussuri River incidents were publicized in 1969 there was speculation that Russia might attempt direct action in Sinkiang, thrusting forward from the carefully prepared positions and cutting it off from the mainland. That Russia attempted no warlike movement or intervention may indicate (besides a wish not to intensify further an already serious confrontation) that the Chinese domination of Sinkiang has been secured and the disaffected tribes are neither as numerous nor anti-Chinese as the Russians like to make out. Their hope of the rise of a separatist movement looking to Moscow for support has faded over the years, and the exodus of nomads has probably proved an embarrassment rather to Russia than to China. A Russian operation against Sinkiang is perfectly feasible but it would be seriously contested by the Chinese who have spent huge sums on improving the defences.

Yet another source of friction between Peking and Moscow is the Mongolian border which separates the Russian-dominated Outer Mongolia and the Chinese autonomous region of Inner Mongolia. Outer Mongolia came under Russian protection in 1911, but its border has never been demarcated and remains an area of contention, although the troubles along it have not been as serious as those which have erupted from time to time along the Ussuri and in Sinkiang. But it was the Mongolian area which first gave the outside world an indication of frontier trouble between the two nations. Occasional clashes were reported from Mongolia in the 'fifties, and it was during this period of intermittent trouble that Russia began to accuse China publicly of encouraging her people to settle in Soviet territory, particularly in the Amur region.

Both sides have tried hard to settle disputed and sparsely popu-lated border areas, but the Chinese seem to have been the more successful, and this annoys the Russians. In the Manchurian border area, however, neither side seems to have had much suc-cess at 'colonization'. The climate is too severe to allow any but a few hardy farmers, seasonal fishermen and the odd smuggler to make much of a living. Because of the difficulties of eking out an existence, there is traditional bad feeling between the Chinese and Russians in the Amur-Ussuri areas. Petty squabbles between farmers and fishermen have been part and parcel of the way of life, and now they serve to exacerbate an already tense and difficult situation. The Chinese also still resent the Russian occupation of Manchuria at the end of the war with Japan. Although the Russians acted on behalf of the Communists and assisted them in many ways, they lost the goodwill of the local inhabitants through rough and rude behaviour. Manchuria has always been the industrial heart of China and before they departed from it the Russians made good pickings from the industrial plant, shipping back thousands of tons of equipment. The Chinese, particularly the local people, have never forgotten this looting, neither have they forgotten earlier Tsarist attempts to annex the area. Had it not been for their defeat at the hands of Japan in 1905, the Russians would undoubtedly have succeeded in gaining Manchuria.

There has rarely been a period in the past century when the Sino-Russian border has enjoyed peace along its whole length. But these local disputes and clashes between the border peoples and then between frontier troops became part of the larger Sino-Soviet quarrel in the 'sixties. The quarrel was ostensibly over ideological differences, but the root of the whole trouble between these countries lies in their traditional suspicion of each other. Russian memories go back to the days of Genghis Khan and the Mongol hordes which laid Russia waste. The Chinese cannot forget Russia's imperial expansion. Communism cloaked their differences only for a time. Stalin never believed that the Chinese Revolution would succeed; he kept a foot in Chiang Kai-shek's camp up to the last days of the Kuomintang. Between Mao and Stalin there was mutual distrust, and Mao's continuing distrust of Russian intentions towards China has affected all his subsequent dealings with Stalin's successors.

The Sino-Russian quarrel is something more than the dispute of neighbours about where to put the garden fence, or than the arguments of two families of Communists over the interpretation of the sacred texts of Marxism; it is the squaring up of traditional enemies who are compulsively driven to seek the opening for a jab at a weak or unguarded spot. Neither can suffer the other to enjoy peace and content. History has placed them in perpetual confrontation.

This confrontation assumed more dangerous proportions in the 'sixties as both sides moved additional troops up to the borders to support the already substantial numbers of frontier units. Along the thousands of miles of frontier there was a tightening of

126

security and a further severe limitation of movement either way. The battle of insults became intense, and there was a good deal of frontier pin-pricking. The Chinese openly denounced the 19th-century treaties as unequal, adding, however, the rider that every outstanding issue could be settled through peaceful negotiation when the time was ripe. The Chinese have kept to this line, though Mao Tse-tung added a sinister note when he detailed to a visiting Japanese delegation the territories the Russians had taken from China. 'We have not yet presented our account for this list,' he declared.

The Russians, for their part, accused Peking of 'artificially fanning nationalist passions and dislike for other peoples'. They rejected the view that the Tsarist treaties were unequal and said they would not re-negotiate their borders in their entirety.

In 1964 a half-hearted attempt was made to take some of the heat out of the affair, and discussions on border issues were started. But the Russians would not budge from their position that the borders had taken shape historically. They said the only issues which could be debated and negotiated were those concerning certain sections of the existing frontier where it was necessary to make it more precise. This was a long way from the Chinese negotiating position and the talks proved empty and futile. Their failure increased the tension between the two countries and by the late 'sixties China was talking in terms of Russia replacing America as her biggest potential enemy. The Cultural Revolution briefly diverted China's attention from the Soviet problem, but it did nothing to alleviate the distrust and hostility the Chinese felt towards Moscow. Indeed, the Revolution had produced hundreds of thousands of young, militant, revolutionary-minded cadres who felt psychologically prepared to take on Russia. As incident succeeded incident in 1969 along the Amur, the Ussuri and in the mountains of Sinkiang, Peking ordered preparations for 'a People's War against aggression'. The *Liberation Army Daily* enunciated the new line when it declared that 'we should not think that by putting politics in command military affairs can be neglected'. This was as good as saying that the time had come to put field and weapon training before political lectures in the PLA's daily routine. The switch was made.

There was a country-wide campaign to improve the already high standards of weapon handling, fieldcraft and hand-to-hand armed and unarmed combat in both the regular and volunteer forces. Efforts were made to increase the strength of the Militia and its minimum age for recruitment was reported to have been reduced to fourteen. More realistically, in view of Russia's nuclear capacity, H-bomb shelters and air raid shelters were built in all the main centres of population. Peking was said to be a veritable warren of underground command posts, tunnels and shelters. PLA aircraft flew back and forth over the cities day and night as the people rehearsed their air raid precautions. Anti-aircraft batteries became a common sight both within and on the outskirts of the cities. Soldiers and civilians alike were given a handbook on 'The evacuation of battle casualties', which gave simple advice on how to dress wounds and perform minor first aid.

Meanwhile the radio and newspapers continued to inveigh against Russia, the passions of the people rising accordingly, and Peking became the centre stage for large-scale and countless anti-Russian solidarity demonstrations. China gave every appearance of being ready to take on a Soviet invasion expected at any moment. The people were clearly united in their readiness and willingness to defend their homeland. In the Politburo and High Command, however, there was no unity but deep divisions and grave disquiet. A group of senior Party members and Army com-manders were disturbed at the heightening of the confrontation with Russia. Defence Minister Lin Piao was among their number. In their view, America presented a threat to China, both im-mediate through its involvement in the Vietnam War, and long-term, through its ringing of China with military bases. They held that United States 'imperialism' posed a bigger danger than Russian 'imperialism' and 'revisionism', and they wanted and pressed for a cooling of the border cauldrons. To some extent they succeeded, but unknown to them and to the rest of the world Mao's handling of the Sino-Soviet argument was the preliminary waltz before the quick-step towards some form of accommodation or *détente* with America.

It may have been that the pro-Russian lobby was responsible for some progress made in 1969 by China and Russia towards settling the Northern Rivers dispute. Mao has a habit, springing from his guerrilla mentality, of bringing on an internal dispute in order to test the strength of the opposition to future moves he is planning but has not yet revealed. He sometimes allows his opponents limited initiatives or manoeuvre as part of his testing of the political will. This pattern of behaviour may explain his decision to agree to the convening of the Joint U.S.S.R./China Commission on River Navigation. The Commission had originally been formed in 1951 and its duties were to regulate navigation on the Amur, Argun, Ussuri and Sungacha, and on Lake Khanka. Both Chinese and Russian ships and inland water traffic have access to these waterways and the Commission met regularly up to 1967 to ensure the safe and orderly passage of all ships.

Because of the increased tension the Commission did not meet in 1968. But on 2 May 1969, Tass announced that the Soviet chairman of the Commission had proposed a meeting to be held in Khabarovsk later in the month. The Chinese agreed that a meeting should be held but rejected the timing. There was some argument over dates and places, but eventually the Commission was able to meet on 18 June, and the sessions continued until 8 August. It was during the course of these talks that the Soviet river worker was killed on Goldinsky Island and his death underlined the need for some new agreement and tighter security precautions to protect civilian lives. When the talks ended neither side revealed much of their content.

Tass said that members of the Commission had signed a protocol recording the agreement of the two sides to carry out during the 1969 navigation season certain measures to improve the shipping situation. But the year was advancing and there was little time left before the onset of winter, so presumably the protocol was meant to continue in force for the following year.

Hsinhua, the official Peking news agency, was hardly more informative on the course of the talks: 'Proceeding in the spirit of making a success of the meeting and settling issues, the Chinese delegation patiently conducted negotiations with the Soviet side on certain specific issues relating to navigation on the boundary rivers between the two countries and signed the minutes of the meeting.'

It was learned later that the Chinese had attempted to widen the Commission's talks from the problems of safe navigation to the more general border issues, but the Soviets would have none of this. The atmosphere in which the talks were held was far from amicable and on at least one occasion the Chinese threatened to withdraw. But, despite all the self-imposed difficulties, progress was made, and after the Commission's sessions there was a noticeable drop in the number of reported riverside clashes. Khabarovsk was therefore a limited success and gave some hope that talks on other issues would also lead to some improvement in the two countries' relations.

The following month, September, saw real political drama injected into the Sino-Russian affair. It came as a direct result of the death of Ho Chi Minh in Hanoi on 3 September. Ho, the President of North Vietnam, had made a deathbed appeal for an end to the divisions between China and Russia and in his political testament had left a pledge that his Party would do its best to help bring about a restoration of unity.

The vital part of the testament, which was read at his funeral, declared:

Having dedicated my entire life to the cause of the revolution, the prouder I am to see the growth of the international Communist and workers' movement, the more deeply I am grieved at the dissensions that are dividing the fraternal Parties. I wish our Party to do its best to contribute effectively to the restoration of unity among fraternal Parties on the basis of Marxism-Leninism and proletarian internationalism, in a manner which accords to the requirements both of the heart and of reason. . . .

No matter whether it was their heads or their hearts which responded to this plea, made more dramatic by the circumstances of its utterance, the leaders in Peking and Moscow acted on Ho's initiative. Chou En-lai flew to Hanoi the day after Ho died. Informed of the contents of Ho's testament, he did not wait for the funeral but returned to Peking the following day. At first Chou's hurried arrival and departure were interpreted in the West as a deliberate Chinese snub to the Russians. It was thought that Chou wanted to get in and out of Hanoi without meeting the Russian delegation which had set out to North Vietnam by the circuitous route of Afghanistan, Pakistan, India and Burma, the only available flight path if China was to be avoided. Subsequent events have since revealed that Chou returned to Peking before Ho's funeral on 8 September, not to deliver a deliberate, obvious and childish snub to Russia's leaders, but for the more constructive purpose of discussing with Mao and the leadership the implications of Ho's appeal. In short: Should there be a meeting with Mr Kosygin? If so, where?

It took the Peking leadership from 5 to 11 September to make up its collective mind. By that time Mr Kosygin was on his way home. A message from Peking reached him when his aircraft landed at Dyushambe, capital of the Tajik SSR. It was an invitation to go to Peking to discuss the crisis. The Russians accepted. The turbo-jet headed east on a 3000-mile leg to Peking. Kosygin had embarked on one of the more extraordinary top-level or summit meetings since the Second World War. No one knows what the Russians were expecting in Peking, but it is hardly likely they were prepared for the reception they got.

At Peking airport there were no fanfares, little ceremonial, just diplomatic formality. The Russian Prime Minister was escorted from his jet to the airport reception lounge for distinguished visitors. And that was as far as he got. He was not invited into the city. Chou En-lai, man of the 20th century but still a Mandarin, met him in the lounge with cold politeness. He quickly made it clear that he was at the airport to listen rather than talk. Kosygin, because of the circumstances, was at a disadvantage, but he tried to make his journey worth while. The atmosphere in the airport lounge could not but be charged with drama. Here, Mao's absence notwithstanding, were some of the leaders of the world's Communist giant states, brought together by the dying wish of a fellow revolutionary, frigidly discussing their problems in the no-man's-land of a sparsely furnished airport reception room. The crisis into which the two nations had been plunged could hardly have been more dramatically highlighted.

The Chinese Red Army

But while there was tension and ill-feeling, there was also hope; for at least the men were meeting and talking. There was a chance that something positive and constructive would emerge from their being closeted together. Would the spark of human contact melt the atmosphere of refrigeration?

After the meeting the official communiqués gave little or no hint of what had taken place. The Russians reported that both sides had explained their positions frankly and held a discussion useful to both. The Chinese were more terse. They simply said that the delegations had had 'a frank conversation', which in Communist parlance usually means disagreement. And since the Chinese did not elaborate it appeared that they had not found the meeting 'useful'.

Later it was learned that the Russians had put forward a five-point plan for resolving the border crisis. It was that the two countries should agree to re-open border talks; that troops on either side of the border should be instructed to avoid opening fire on each other; that the two countries should agree to withdraw their troops a certain distance from the border; that they should stop press and radio criticism of each other; that they should agree to work towards the restoration of trade and economic ties. When the Russians had leaked their proposals, the Chinese revealed that at the talks their position had been that in order to reduce tension along the border the two sides should first reach agreement on provisional measures for maintaining the *status quo* along the border, for averting armed conflict and for disengagement. The Chinese were clearly not prepared to go as far as the Russians in the attempt to bring back a measure of normality in their relationship.

The immediate result of the airport talks was a drop in the amount of anti-Chinese propaganda put out by the Russians. This was done as a sign of Moscow's goodwill. The Chinese did not respond. If anything, they increased the intensity of their verbal assault on the Russians and continued with their defensive war preparations. But there was some relaxation in the tension which had gripped the border regions for months on end.

It appeared that China was being bull-headed about the situation. But what the Chinese say and what they do are very often widely different things. On 7 October they suddenly announced that it had been agreed to hold talks at deputy ministerial level, with the object of finding a solution to the dispute on the border regions. Russia, somewhat taken aback at the possibly precipitate Chinese announcement, quickly followed by announcing their own agreement to the talks. Peking then released a long and detailed statement of its position. It was a tough document; in it Peking seemed to be saying that the decision to enter into talks should not be taken as a sign that negotiations would be approached from a position of weakness.

The main points of the statement, which was repeated endlessly on the radio, and printed and reprinted in newspapers and journals, were that there must be a ceasefire along the whole border and a pull-back of troops from disputed 'hot' areas; Russia must recognize the illegality of the 19th-century treaties by which she had acquired Chinese territory, and territory occupied by the Russians and not covered by treaties must be given back. Once Moscow had agreed to these points and carried out what was required of her, then a mutual and satisfactory agreement on the new borders could be negotiated.

One passage, which typifies Chinese thinking, runs as follows:

Precisely because the Soviet Government continues to persist in its expansionist attitude many disputed areas have been created along the Sino-Soviet border, and this has become the root cause of the tension on the border.

The Chinese Government has never hidden the fact that there exist irreconcilable differences of principle between China and the Soviet Union and that the struggle of principle between them will continue for a long period of time. But this should not prevent China and the Soviet Union from maintaining normal State relations on the basis of the Five Principles of Peaceful Co-Existence. The Chinese Government has consistently held that the Sino-Soviet boundary question should be settled peacefully and that, even if it cannot be settled for the time being, the *status quo* of the border should be maintained and there should definitely be no resort to the use of force.

There is no reason whatsoever for China and the Soviet Union to go to war over the boundary question.

The Chinese Red Army

The first paragraph of the above is contentious, but the rest is a remarkably frank assessment of the situation and a realistic attitude to ways of at least bringing some relief. And it offered real hope where up to a few weeks previously there had been little hope at all and the menace of a nuclear conflict had seemed to be growing.

On the latter question, the document had this to say:

China is developing nuclear weapons for defence and in order to break the nuclear monopoly. The Chinese Government has declared solemnly on many occasions that, at no time and under no circumstances, will China be the first to use nuclear weapons. It is both ridiculous and absurd to vilify China as intending to launch a nuclear war.

But, at the same time, China will never be intimidated by the threat of war including the threat of nuclear war. Should a handful of war maniacs dare to raid China's strategic sites in defiance of world condemnation, that will be war! That will be aggression! And the 700 million Chinese people will rise up in resistance and use revolutionary war to eliminate the war of aggression!

Thus, China's position as she went in for the talks – they began in Peking on 20 October 1969 – was tough but realistic. Her position has not changed one iota since the issuing of the 7000-word document. The talks, which have continued on and off ever since, have made little progress. Russia is just as dogmatic. But late in 1971 Moscow did attempt to break the deadlock by offering to accept the international principle on river borders. Until then she had insisted that her Amur-Ussuri border ran along the Chinese river banks and not down the centre of the main channel. This shift in the Soviet position meant conceding hundreds of river islands to the Chinese, including Damansky Island. In effect this offer was not so generous as it first appeared. Apart from Russia's agreeing to conform to a world-wide practice, she was agreeing also to the *status quo* or line of actual control. In other words she was giving up what in most cases she did not possess, and the islands she did possess were more of a tactical nuisance than an advantage. As it was, the offer came to nothing. China rejected it as insufficient to bring about a general border settlement. We have seen that China is not out to recover all the territory lost to the Tsars, but she is very much concerned to get back territory lost through subsequent Russian incursions. In particular she wants restored to her the strategically valuable Pamir Plateau in the west, into which the Russians have advanced a couple of hundred miles. In other areas she is prepared to take into account the interests of local inhabitants especially in those zones where the local inhabitants have neither ethnic nor cultural affinity with the Han people. She wants and insists upon an overall settlement, but the Russians, as is shown by their river border offer, are prepared to make only minimal concessions over the maximum amount of time.

Soviet delaying tactics are allied with their global propaganda strategy which is based on the theme of the peril China presents to world peace and stability. Moscow uses this scare, presenting China as an expansionist and aggressive nation which needs to be contained, in order to cause apprehension in the West and in non-Communist Asia. Until recently it brought forth a responsive echo. But Russia's nervousness towards China, even towards Asia generally, goes further and deeper than anything of the like felt in America or Europe. Russia believes sincerely that since the days of the Mongols her historic role has been to defend Europe against the eruptions of Eastern peoples. But this self-imposed role of defender of civilization has often masked a policy of predatory incursion into the Eastern regions. Russia is in fact a Eurasian power, but she admits the reality only when it suits her purposes.

Russia genuinely fears the East and its peoples, and makes little distinction between them. She has never forgotten the débâcle of 1905 when she ran up against the emergent Japanese nation. Chinese, Japanese, Mongols – all are alike to Russia in that they present a threat to her security. Tsarist and Soviet encroachments eastward were designed and executed as much for defence as for territorial and commercial gain. The farther flung her frontiers, the safer Russia feels.

The Kremlin also believes that the China threat will become more real as the years go by; that a Chinese economic threat is just as big as the military one. This explains in part the determined Russian drive to win over and gain Japanese, other Asian and European economic 'friends'. In short Russia is attempting to get an edge now in order to blunt a threat she may have to face in decades to come.

Russia's public posture towards China was demonstrated in all its many facets in a speech by Communist Party chief, Leonid Brezhnev, in December 1972, when he accused the Peking leadership of seeking 'the greatest possible damage to the Soviet Union'. 'What does Peking's foreign policy amount to today?' he asked. 'It amounts to absurd claims on Soviet territory, to malicious slander of the Soviet social and political system and our peace-loving foreign policy.'

Brezhnev went on to declare that other objectives pursued by the Chinese were to split the socialist camp, to incite the Third World against Moscow, and to seek common cause with any anti-Soviet state, no matter what its ideological line. He then dismissed as impossible to understand Peking's charge that it was under 'a threat from the north'.

Whether or not the Kremlin leadership can understand it, the Chinese do feel threatened, and with cause. The Russian military build-up along the borders has been going on since 1966 when the Politburo decided that China posed a long-term threat to Russia's security. Numerous permanent facilities have been built for troops in the border regions, and half a million men in forty-nine divisions, one-third of them armoured divisions, are now deployed along the borders. In 1968 there were just fifteen divisions spread over the whole length of the border. In addition, of course, there are the numerous missile sites in Siberia and Mongolia. No estimate can be made of their numbers. It can be safely assumed, however, that there are more than enough missiles targeted to take out the major centres of population and China's own missile sites.

The Soviet High Command, despite its preponderance in hardware, doubts whether Russia could fight a short, sharp war with China and achieve complete victory through a massive, knock-out blow. The generals are apprehensive about getting bogged down in a long campaign with the Chinese fighting their own-style People's War. Any Soviet attack on China would of necessity have to begin with a pre-emptive nuclear strike followed by a thrust into Sinkiang to cut off China's own nuclear facilities and launching sites, and a drive on Peking and into the great northern plain to seal off her industrial capacity. But this would still be insufficient to lay China low. She would fall back south and west and the PLA would immediately begin the guerrilla campaign. Success would thus elude Russia, and China would still win, even if it took another hundred years. But the possibility of Russia attempting such a war diminishes year by year as China's nuclear arm gains steadily in strength and hitting power. In an invasion of Russia the Chinese would face similar problems to those the Russian generals have considered. So there is a stand-off, and the two nations have got themselves into a situation in which they are neither at war nor are they at peace.

The intensity of the confrontation varies from time to time. The fires stoked by both sides in 1969 died down somewhat the following year, but Lin Piao's reported contacts with the Russians before his death added new fuel to the glowing embers. Again the quarrel blazed in December 1972, when Soviet troops clashed with Chinese in the Kazakhstan area and lost five men killed. The Chinese were also said to have killed a number of shepherds and stolen a flock of sheep. The Russians were reported to have taken a Chinese prisoner. Peking denied any knowledge of the incident, the first reported since 1969; local Chinese authorities disclaimed any responsibility for the clash on the grounds that whatever happened was probably the result of a bandit raid. This may well have been true as the area is teeming with nomads and warring tribes who have no respect for the relatively modern notion of borders and nation states. But the incident did nothing to help the tense border situation; and indeed it demonstrates how local, traditional patterns of behaviour can have a much wider influence and impact. It was noticeable, however, that Moscow was ready to play up the killing, while Peking behaved in exactly the opposite manner.

Beyond their immediate borders the conflict between the two

countries is being waged on the diplomatic front. Russia is making strong efforts to encircle China with allies not necessarily of the same ideological persuasion. She is assiduously courting South-East Asian countries, Japan and India. The latter is now supported by Moscow in her own border quarrel with China. Indeed, Moscow has taken the initiative in resurrecting the dormant dispute, and in the January 1973 issue of the authoritative quarterly journal, *Problems of the Far East*, Mr G. V. Matveev firmly laid the blame for the dispute and the 1962 war on China's shoulders. The likely reason for this Russian return to an old problem (possibly not totally welcomed in New Delhi) is that a strong lobby in India is now advocating that Moscow should be ditched in favour of Peking – Asians coming to terms with Asians. This has alarmed the Moscow leadership and the courting of Mrs Gandhi is being carried on more zealously than before. There are those in India and other Asian countries, however, who resent being used by Russia as pawns in the power chess-game with China. Non-alignment and neutrality are more than slogans for those who wish to keep out of either ideological corner or just, for the time being, to keep their diplomatic options open.

Russian strategy therefore is on two levels. First, a high state of military preparedness along the borders and, second, the encirclement of China or her fencing in through diplomacy. Peking's answer to this is to be ready to fight a defensive war should Russia ever attempt to try conclusions while going on to the diplomatic offensive. Her entry into the United Nations has given her an international forum which she has so far used mainly to harry, harass and counteract Soviet diplomacy. She is also seeking new friends in Europe, particularly Britain whom she sees as the future leader of the European Economic Community. The Chinese are much agitated lest any political and military *détente* in Europe should provide Russia with an opportunity of applying new pressure in the East and on the border questions. China believes Britain to be in accord with her view that distrust should inform all dealings with Moscow, that Russia understands only strength and respects only those who are clearly prepared to use it if necessary. The Peking Politburo is convinced that with a strong

British influence in the Common Market there will be no disposition to edge the Community closer to Russia than it is at the moment.

So, while their common border problems remain in deadlock, both China and Russia would a-wooing go to gather if not friends of a like mind then neutrals biased in their favour. The exercise is not particularly productive for either side.

What of the future? The likelihood is that Soviet policy, verbal vitriol against Peking and honeyed words to those of possible anti-Chinese persuasion, will remain much the same, certainly until Mao goes. The Russian leaders will wait patiently and hopefully for a new leadership to emerge, a leadership perhaps more pragmatic and willing to adjust more to the Soviet way of thinking. The basic issues of the dispute are unlikely to be resolved this century, but there may well develop a more realistic 'live and let live' approach. As one American observer has said, the two countries are likely to be 'strained and restrained' in their relationship, both waiting, soberly and rationally, to see what the future brings.

But the future is more likely to bring satisfaction to the Chinese than to the Russians. The Chinese will be more prepared to wait it out, for everything comes to the Chinese who waits. China has made a national asset of time and patience; she has an instinctive ability to appreciate the dimensions of time in relation to seemingly urgent problems of the moment. To exaggerate, but not overmuch, the Chinese would not think it particularly odd if the final signatures were to be added today to Magna Carta or the American Constitution. There is an old story about the Chinese diplomat who was asked at a Western cocktail party his views of the effects and influence of the French Revolution on subsequent European history. After considering the question for some time, he said with finality: 'It is too early to say.'

Although Russia and China will in the years to come apply pressure points where they think some advantage can be gained, they will allow for the passage of time to bring about circumances stand an atmosphere conducive to negotiation.

There is a line of thought which says that, for all their bared teeth and the years of acrimony, there is a deep and fundamental desire among both Chinese and Russians to reach an agreement, to solve amicably all their problems and differences; that there is no question of either of them taking their dispute to the point at which war would become inevitable; that this is in its essentials a lovers' quarrel and that third parties will interfere at their peril. This view is tenable only if one believes that Communism has for ever supplanted the natural behaviour patterns, psychology and thought processes of the essential Chinese. The gathering evidence is that it has not.

No, the Chinese will wait upon time because it is in their nature to do so. The Russians will wait because they have a respect, born partly out of fear, for Chinese ability and capacity. A Frenchman at the court of Tsar Nicolas in the 1840s once reported to Paris that among the St Petersburg diplomatic corps there was a belief that it was Russia's destiny to expand into Asia and there smash itself into two. The Kremlin keepers of Eurasian Russia bear this same thought in mind today, and perhaps more than any other single factor it restrains them from taking military action to resolve their perpetual China dilemma.

In time, in a very long time, the Russians may learn not to fear China, to appreciate that the world's oldest civilization is unlikely to end itself and the civilizations of other peoples in a nuclear holocaust. Perhaps, too, the Chinese will find themselves able to accommodate some portion of the Soviet negotiating position. But for the moment in the Peking/Moscow equation there are too many unknown factors for any positive answers to be supplied about the future.

Meanwhile, across the mountains and deserts of Sinkiang, over the vast reaches of Mongolia and along the Amur, Argun and Ussuri Rivers, the border watches go on, and will go on, day and night, year in and year out. From time to time men will die in sudden, savage, senseless fire fights. And when they do, be they dressed in Chinese olive-green or Russian drab brown, the world will again, as it did in 1969, hold its breath.

THE ARMY AND POLITICS

We must emphasize politics. Our Army is an
Army in the service of politics . . . and
politics must guide the military and day-to-day
work – *Lin Piao*

The Chinese Communist Party climbed to power through its
military arm, the PLA, and in the years immediately following
the civil war it was the Army which secured Party rule. 'Political
power grows out of the barrel of a gun,' said Mao, but since 1949
the Peking regime has been deeply troubled from time to time by
the question of who should exercise the greater control over the
gun – the Army or the Party. In other words: Whose finger should
be on the trigger? The Party's continuing problem has been that it
needs a strong Army for defence and internal security, but one not
so powerful that it can dominate the leadership and present itself
to the people as an alternative to civilian rule. The Army has to have
the weapons of course, but the Party wants the key to the armoury
door in its collective waistcoat pocket.

Mao laid it down in his Yenan wilderness days that the gun
must never slip from the controlling hands of the Party, and this in
practice meant that the PLA had to be subservient to its wishes
and dictates. This is unexceptionable doctrine, and for the
Chinese it worked well enough until the 'fifties, when after prolonged arguments and tensions behind the closed doors of the
Politburo the disagreements between the military and Party
hierarchy began to be voiced in public, leading to the first Army/
Party crisis which Mao resolved in 1959 with a purge among the
High Command. There was another crisis situation in 1970–71 and
it ended in the death of Defence Minister Lin Piao and yet
another shake-up at the top.

The uneasy relationship between the Army and the Party has
resulted in the PLA suffering from a series of internal stresses and

strains which must have reduced its effectiveness and combat preparedness at various critical periods during the past twenty years.

The testing of civilian and military wills has been an inevitable development in the People's Republic because Mao, 'the great helmsman', has held an unswerving course for his goal of continuing, self-perpetuating revolution. The 'right to rebel' of the masses, which resulted in upheavals like the Great Leap Forward and the Cultural Revolution, has been regarded with a jaundiced eye by the more conservative military. Mao's guerrilla mentality and his firm adherence to the concepts of the People's War, in which men are regarded as more important than weapons, have dismayed many commanders who, in a nuclear and missile age, doubt the validity of the doctrine which holds that 'in war, man is the determining element'. At the same time, Mao has had his supporters among the PLA; they have usually been men of the Long March generation but have also included younger apostles of the guerrilla gospel. These two groups, professionals and guerrillas, have been in conflict for nearly two decades. Their dispute has been termed the 'Red versus expert' row.

The professionals or 'experts' have also clashed seriously with the Party, and the disagreements have issued from ideological matters which have impinged upon questions of military modernization, professionalism and strategy. In arguing their case, however, the generals have appeared to be questioning the wisdom of Mao and uniting against the Party leadership. The power structure in Peking produced the logical consequence that the Chairman's views prevailed and the Army found itself under a cloud. But Mao's major domestic initiatives have brought about chaotic conditions in which the Party has had to turn to the PLA as the only body capable of restoring order and bringing back stability; moreover, an organization which commands such wide and enormous esteem among the people cannot be kept out of official favour for an undue length of time. Displeasure has been followed by touching reconciliation.

The origins of the Army/Party troubles are to be found in the years after the Korean War, which had revealed grave deficiencies in the PLA's weaponry, equipment and organization. The

142

fanatical courage of the troops and their high standard of training had not been sufficient to overcome these weaknesses. Senior officers had realized the need for modernization after the victory over the Kuomintang and a start had been made, with Russian help, in 1950. The Korean War slowed the process up but did not lessen the determination of the High Command to bring about changes. For instance, at the height of the war, Chu Teh, the Army's commander-in-chief, told the nation in a radio broadcast on the PLA's 24th anniversary that the Army was transforming itself from a purely land force to one with land, naval and air arms with various kinds of modern technical equipment for waging co-ordinated warfare. He went on: 'Our troops must be active in studying the techniques [of co-ordinated warfare] and must absorb the highly advanced military science of the Soviet Union.'

To bring this about, said Chu Teh, a three-point programme was to be carried out: an increase in the size of the armed forces, a strengthening of the Army with technical weapons, and intensive political indoctrination – 'the whole Army must continue to conduct profound political training'. He hardly mentioned Korea.

The veterans from the peninsula battles were more concerned with weaponry than political training. They were impressed with the firepower and mobility of Western and Russian units and they argued that the PLA would need to be supplied with better artillery and more tanks if it was ever to engage again in war with the West or take on the Nationalist forces on Taiwan. The Army's case was accepted, although the need to turn to Russia for help and expertise was not universally popular among Party leaders. Now the Army of the Soviet Union became the one on which the Chinese set out to base their own. Russian advisers arrived in the country in increasing numbers and they pushed through an extensive programme of modernization, re-organization and re-training. The men from the Military Mission delivered their lectures on time, but their masters in Moscow were not so punctual with their deliveries of tanks, guns and jet fighters, and this had the side effect of delaying the standardization of PLA weapons and equipment.

Within the limits they were allowed by their secret directives,

143

the Russian officers made a reasonable job of their by no means easy task. It has been argued that the Red Army of the 'thirties would not have survived the Nationalist assaults and campaigns if the officer corps had not had earlier the benefit of serving and learning alongside Nationalist officers in the days of the Communist-Kuomintang alliance. And if it had not been for the Russians, it is unlikely that the PLA on its own would have achieved in so relatively short a time the high degree of professionalism and modernization it was able to exhibit by the mid-fifties.

This Russianizing process was further accelerated in 1954 when Marshal Peng Teh-huai, the former commander-in-chief in Korea, replaced Chu Teh as Minister of Defence. Peng was an admirer of the armed forces of the Soviet Union and of Russian technology, and he intensified efforts to get Russian assistance and know-how. He reduced the amount of political indoctrination the PLA had to undergo, and he ushered in internal changes which included giving the PLA a properly defined system of ranks and appropriate salaries. Officers and men were given smart, tailored uniforms with rank insignia and lots of gold braid for generals and the marshals. Even batmen made a brief, if tentative, appearance on the scene!

This emergence of a new model army with all the trappings of a conventional capitalist army disturbed many of the old guard who had been brought up in the revolutionary tradition, and a military generation gap began to appear. But the modernizers were in the ascendant and the guerrilla-minded faction kept themselves to themselves – and waited their chance.

The men of the People's War knew they had one great ally in Mao. He, perhaps more than anybody, was unhappy at the emergence of a military caste, something completely alien to him and his ideology; and the Army's persistent clamour for new and better weapons, its open admiration of almost everything Russian, he accepted on sufferance. He resisted the PLA's demands for missiles and nuclear warheads for a considerable period, dismissing atomic bombs as 'paper tigers'. The professionals did not attempt to hide their scorn.

144

And then the unexpected happened. In a surprise turn-about, Mao decided there was something to be said for nuclear weapons after all. The most likely explanation is that he was forced to bow to the high-pressure arguments of the powerful Marshal Peng and his similar-minded colleagues. Russia was approached and in October 1957 Premier Nikita Khrushchev offered the Chinese a sample atomic bomb. Mao now started talking in terms of 'the east wind prevailing over the west wind', and the mirage of Soviet nuclear help also probably inspired a new aggressiveness towards Taiwan. In the late summer of 1958 Communist batteries opened fire on the Nationalist-held offshore islands of Quemoy and Matsu. But Khrushchev's gesture had been half-hearted and he soon attempted to renege on the nuclear agreement. Peng was dismayed, and Mao must have realized that he had made a mistake in ever trusting Moscow's word. Under the influence of Peng and the professionals he had ignored all his previous experience of dealing with Russia and had believed he would get his atomic bomb. At this stage, however, he was still anxious to see the nuclear co-operation agreement fulfilled, and a direct request was made to Khrushchev for the speedy delivery of nuclear weapons.

Sino-Russian relations had already started on their downward path and in 1958 Khrushchev suggested the unacceptable – that China could have the weapons so long as the Soviet Union maintained complete control over them. The arguments went back and forth with a steady trade in harsh words until the eventual total breakdown of relations between the two countries ended any chance of Russia's assisting China into the nuclear age.

Peng and his senior colleagues were appalled by this turn of events. So much so that Peng is believed to have made a direct and personal appeal to Moscow for the honouring of the nuclear agreement. The Army was not just worried about losing its nuclear arm. The PLA was heavily dependent on the Soviet Union for a wide range of weaponry and logistic equipment, even fuel for the air force, which would take years for China's industry to provide. Without Russia where could the PLA turn?

But as the PLA High Command debated the consequences of making Russia an ideological enemy, Mao went back to his old familiar line: Man was greater than any weapon that might be used against him.

This was a clear indication that the PLA was in deep trouble. But Peng had never given ground willingly, and he wasn't going to do so now. The scene was set for a clash of the titans. The crunch came, however, as a result of events in other spheres than military – events which had been taking place at the same time as the nuclear dispute with Russia.

In an attempt to apply guerrilla thinking and methods in the economic field, Mao had launched his Great Leap Forward in 1958. The idea was to mobilize the people in a great mass-revolutionary effort with the object of achieving a breakthrough in industrial and agricultural production. According to Mao, all obstacles and difficulties in whatever field – military, economic, cultural, sport – can be overcome if the people are properly organized, if they have the will to succeed. The Great Leap Forward turned out to be a big jump backward to economic disaster. Conditions in the country soon became chaotic. To Mao the reason for the collapse of his grandiose plan was obvious: since the strategy could not be wrong, the blame for failure lay with those charged with carrying it out; and that meant the Party cadres and the bureaucrats. The PLA also caught the backlash. Mao was aware that the military had stood aloof from his brain-child; the officers near to Peng had not been to any great pains to hide their view that the Great Leap was a ridiculous, wasteful and dangerous venture, and bad for the Army since the soldiers were restless as they heard stories from their villages, towns and provinces, of famine and starvation and of the breakdown of essential services. Natural disasters had worsened the chaos created by the Great Leap, but the PLA was in no mood for excuses. Some units were reported to be on the verge of mutiny.

Mao was now facing a crisis of confidence, which deepened in August 1959, when the ever-forceful Peng denounced Mao for creating country-wide disorder and crippling the Army with 'anti-professional measures'. There was never a time when the Chairman needed friends more; he also needed the PLA. The question was: how to get the Army on his side? In September he took the dangerous step, but the only one really open to him, of dismissing Peng and a host of senior officers. But before taking this drastic action he had ensured for himself the support of some powerful, 'old faithful' allies, including the venerable, but still formidable, Chu Teh.

To replace the disgraced Peng the Chairman chose the trusted, guerrilla-minded Marshal Lin Piao, who was given the job of moulding a new PLA, one more to Mao's liking and one which in the future could be used as a military-political instrument capable of assisting with radical programmes along the lines of the Great Leap Forward. In Mao's view the officers had had their say and their own way for far too long. Their emergence into a professional, articulate and motivated body had been anathema to him. He believed they had been responsible for taking the Army out of the mainstream of Chinese life. Lin's job was to put the PLA back where it belonged – among the people, and under the firm control and guidance of the Party leadership and machine.

But Mao did not get things all his own way. If he was to have the Army as an extra power base for himself, then the Army would co-operate but only if he too gave concessions. A deal or agreement was reached whereby the Army accepted political indoctrination and a possible political role in the years ahead in return for a programme of re-equipment with new and improved infantry weapons, necessary because of the Sino-Soviet split and the drying up of Russian aid. It is also probable that the PLA extracted a promise from Mao that China's nuclear effort would go ahead unimpeded, with the required funds, and that the whole nuclear question, a politically sensitive one, would be kept out of Party politics and the public forum.

The guidelines established, Lin immediately went to work to assert his authority over an Army badly shaken by the purge of Marshal Peng and his colleagues and still in a state of unrest at the way the country had been plunged into economic chaos. But Lin had to maintain a fine balance between the professionals – a strong element, despite the dismissals – and those who supported the new Mao line and believed that politics had to be re-emphasized and military thinking re-channelled into the old guerrilla culverts. Lin had to play, for a time at least, both strong man and diplomat. To assist him in his enormous task, General Lo Jui-ching was appointed Chief of Staff. Lo, a friend of Lin's from the Long March days, had once been political commissar in a division commanded by the rising young officer. Later he had developed a taste for security and police work.

One of Lin's first actions was to strengthen the Party's control over the PLA by giving greater power to the Army's Political Department which soon became the headquarters for all internal political activities within the Army and for all civil-military programmes. This move was designed to eradicate for ever the danger of the PLA appearing to be an alternative to the Party as the country's ruling body. The Party was never again to be challenged in the way Marshal Peng had contrived to challenge it.

There then followed a series of major reforms, the majority of which were laid down and detailed at a meeting of the Military Affairs Commission, the supreme Army policy-making body, in October 1960. They included the placing of Army/Party committees under the supervision of local civilian Party committees as well as the Party committees of the Military Regions. This organizational change put the PLA in an unshakeable Party grip and opened the way for a greater degree of political teaching, study and indoctrination. Political commissars now ranked in importance with regimental and divisional officers, and these men led the way in making the PLA a training and recruiting ground for Party members. The idea behind this was that the Army should provide China with 'revolutionary heirs' to the Long March generation so that the heritage of Mao and others would be in safe keeping. Not all soldiers aspired to Party membership, but those who did and later obtained it found themselves very often given important posts on the various civilian committees when they eventually left the Army.

By the end of 1963 the PLA was being held up to the country as a model Maoist organization, an example for others to follow. It was extolled for its ideological purity, its correct thinking, revolutionary spirit and dedication to Maoist principles. Indeed, it was the PLA which gave birth to that feature of life in China in the 'sixties – the study and recitation of the Thoughts of Mao. After the short war and stunning victory over India in 1962, Lin could claim that the bringing back of politics into the Army had in no way affected its ability to wage war, but had actually increased its morale and fighting spirit. In 1964 a massive publicity campaign was launched across the country with the slogan: 'Learn from the PLA'. The hope was that the Party bureaucracy and organizations, discredited in Mao's eyes by their Great Leap failures, would shake themselves up and follow the trail blazed by the Army. The campaign was not a success. The Party machine did not take the hint to put its house in Maoist order.

Meanwhile controversy had again broken out between the professionals and the guerrillas. The immediate cause is not known, but it can be reasonably assumed that the Vietnam War had much to do with it. The professionals were concerned that the new and almost total emphasis on politics was having a detrimental effect on the Army's fighting ability. Their worries came to the surface as the Vietnam War mounted with growing American involvement and as contingency plans were made for China's possible participation.

But Mao and Lin were holding the Army up as the supreme example of right thinking and training, and they were not prepared to suffer disruption from this quarter. The chief spokesman of the rebels was, surprisingly, General Lo, the Chief-of-Staff. He was a recent convert to the modernizers, but he did not carry anything like the weight of the former rebel, Marshal Peng, and his departure into obscurity, along with a number of other likeminded officers, excited little outward passion.

With these last remaining professionals cleared out, Lin was now ready to make another gesture towards Maoist purity and internal democracy. He abolished all ranks within the PLA; gold braid and insignia disappeared and uniforms went back to revolutionary simplicity.

And once again the superiority of the soldier over weapons was emphasized. On the 20th anniversary celebrations of China's victory over Japan, Lin declared:

The poorly armed have defeated the better armed. People's armed forces, beginning with only primitive weapons – swords, spears, rifles, hand grenades – have in the end defeated the imperialist forces armed with modern aircraft, tanks, heavy artillery, and atom bombs. Guerrilla forces have ultimately defeated regular armies. Amateurs who were never trained in any military schools have eventually defeated professional graduates from military academies.

—Later in his speech he went back to the same point:

However highly developed modern weapons and technical equipment may be and however complicated the methods of modern war, in the final analysis the outcome of a war will be decided by the sustained fighting of the ground forces, by fighting at close quarters on battlefields, by the political consciousness of the men, by their courage and spirit of sacrifice.

This 'Think guerrilla' campaign was backed by the Party papers and journals, and all over China soldiers and civilians began to practise hand-to-hand combat and self-defence techniques. The 'Reds' had the 'experts' under the heel of their boots and they meant to keep them there. In another move to bolster the PLA's campaign, hundreds of 'soldier heroes' were designated. These were men, it was claimed, who were the living embodiment of Maoist ideals in both the martial arts and political thinking. Later whole units were singled out for special awards. The PLA was overflowing with righteousness.

Mao at about this time gave his view of the PLA in the following words:

The People's Liberation Army should be a great school. In this great school our army men should learn politics, military affairs and culture. They can also engage in agricultural production and side occupations, run some medium or small factories and manufacture a number of products . . . They can also do mass work and take part in the socialist education movement in the factories and villages . . .

But all this propaganda on the virtues of the PLA failed in its desired object of revolutionizing other sectors of the country's organizational structure and by 1965 Mao had decided that a frontal attack was needed. The Party machine had stubbornly refused to take notice of the changed directions and radical policies he was advocating; the disenchantment in the top Party echelons had spread rather than diminished after the failure of the Great Leap Forward, but Mao was more certain than ever of the correctness of his approach. He decided to remove the powerful stumbling blocks of cadres and bureaucrats, and began his offensive on these rigid bastions secure in the knowledge that the PLA leadership was firmly behind him and that the Army could be called upon if or when needed. China now experienced the phenomenon of the Cultural Revolution, the bursting open of a political-revolutionary volcano which rocked and shook the country to its very foundations and reduced the Great Leap Forward by comparison to a minor earth tremor.

The PLA did not play a conspicuous part in the early stages of the Revolution. It stood on the sidelines, accepted the praise and adulation bestowed on it, watched as first intellectuals and then powerful men like Liu Shao-chi, the head of state, were attacked and toppled, and as the centre stage of the drama was occupied by rampaging Red Guards, the bannermen of the new radicalism. Lin Piao even attended Red Guard rallies and on one occasion urged them 'to strike down and bombard the headquarters of the handful of powerholders who are taking the capitalist path'.

On 1 January 1967, the Revolution entered a new and vicious stage when the Red Guards were officially encouraged to take the struggle into the farms and factories. They did so with a vengeance, and threw the country into even greater disorder. But by now the public were growing weary of the fiery young militants, and workers in industry and on the land began to resist them. The Revolution developed into a contest between two opposing camps – the forces of disorder and destruction in the form of the raging radicals, and the forces of order in the uniforms of factory workers and farm workers who wanted to return to normality. It also became clear that many in the High Command of the PLA were far from happy with the conduct of the Red Guards and they began to gather support for action to stop their activities.

By September 1967 the country had got so out of hand that a halt had to be called. Mao's wife, Chiang Ching, the mentor and inspirer of the young revolutionaries, on the 5th of the month delivered a warning to the Guards. The time for violent struggle was over, she said. The PLA had anticipated her and had already taken over civil police functions by assuming control of the Public Security Bureau in Peking, and many regional commanders had acted on their own initiative and clamped down on the Guards' activities.

The forces of law and order, in the shape of the PLA, slowly but inexorably brought the Revolution to a close. By late 1968 the Army was carrying out many Government functions and was heavily represented on the new revolutionary committees which had been set up to replace the shattered Party and administrative organizations.

During the final stages of the Revolution the PLA had not been without its own troubles, and a group of moderates, including the Acting Chief-of-Staff, Yang Cheng-wu, were dismissed after coming under attack from the radicals and suffering the indignities of wall-poster accusations. The Army shrugged off this trouble and emerged from the upheaval without a blot on its reputation.

The Revolution brought the PLA directly into the political process in China. It did not act arbitrarily, but was invited to involve itself as the young militants stampeded out of control. For instance, in the summer of 1968 the Red Guards rose again after a breathing space and fought out battles between themselves. Mao, who by this time was convinced that the country had gone 'red' and that to allow the Guards further leniency would crack the country wide open and bring down everything and everyone in civil war, not only ordered them to disband but allowed the Army to enforce his wishes in areas where the Guards were still belligerent.

Lin's men brought back a semblance of order to China, and because of their invited intervention in national affairs could now make their influence felt at the policy-making level in Peking. The breakdown of the economy and public services also forced the Army to shoulder a wide range of civil duties. Regional commanders were given powers and responsibilities which had previously been the prerogative of the Party headquarters in the capital, and the latter inevitably suffered from a lessening of authority.

The Army did not seek its new role, but it came to it because of the earlier decision to transform the organization into one on the Maoist model, and because it was the only trusted body capable of saving the nation from foundering from revolutionary excess. The result of all this was a major change in the country's structure of power, but it was of short duration.

The Cultural Revolution catapulted Lin Piao into a position of power second only to Mao. In 1966, at the height of the disturbances, he was described as the Chairman's 'dearest comrade' and was made Vice-Chairman of the Party. Three years later the Ninth Congress of the Party confirmed him as Mao's chosen heir. The only question-mark against Lin was whether he would live to succeed the Chairman for although he was some ten years younger he had never enjoyed good health. As it turned out, Lin has not survived Mao, and his mysterious death in 1971 plunged the Government and Army into a new crisis, a political maelstrom which is still whirling beneath the seemingly placid surface of the Peking scene.

Lin disappeared from view in the autumn of 1971 and some eight months later it was revealed that he had been killed on 12 September in a Trident plane crash in Mongolia while attempting to escape from China after a failed plot to overthrow Mao.

He is now accused of most of the crimes in the Communist book (Chinese version), and there are as many theories on what he was really up to as there are grains of rice in a New Year eating bowl. What is certain is that the defence chief was involved in a conspiracy, the intention of which was to make him leader of the Chinese people, and the machinations of which probably involved pushing the Chairman upstairs into a meaningless position where he could still be revered by the people but would have no executive power.

A report released by the Taiwan Intelligence Service in August 1972, and which is accepted by authorities on China as a reasonable interpretation of events, says that the growing animosity between Mao and Lin broke out into the open at the Second Plenum of the Ninth Party Congress in August–September 1970. Mao is said to have accused Lin and the generals of carrying out

153

underground activities against him and staging 'a surprise attack' against his leadership. Lin was also accused of developing the theory of genius as it applied to Mao, something which had annoyed Mao intensely but which at the time he had been powerless to halt. Mao's attacks on Lin were oblique, guerrilla-style, but to those whose ears were attuned by years spent in the forward political listening posts the message came through loud and clear. The stealthy encroachment on the leadership and the sapping of Mao's position had been discovered. It may well have been that Mao was giving a generous hint to his old and trusted friend not to be too anxious for the succession and to tread carefully. Lin would have done well at this time to have adopted the methods and style of Chou En-lai, the permanent Mandarin, but for reasons we are unlikely ever to discover the defence chief over-reacted. Fevered, perhaps, by a guilty conscience, he increased the tempo of his plotting.

With the benefit of hindsight and the scraps of information emanating from Peking it is now possible to see that Lin had been getting himself into trouble from the days when he first promulgated the Little Red Book of Mao's Thoughts and developed the cult of personality. The exaggerated praise of Mao, his glorification on earth, may have been part of an intricate game to bring the Chairman to an earthly end. This is the official line and Mao, the old campaigner, claims to have spotted what Lin and his friends were up to. Or was Mao being too suspicious? Did he over-react and precipitate Lin into a conspiracy he had only been pondering until the Second Plenum, for it is possible to believe that Lin was genuine in his admiration – even adoration – of Mao.

The charges against Lin range from his alleged desire to see a return of capitalism to his being a Left extremist, helping to push the Cultural Revolution in directions Mao never intended. Mao now claims that he never wanted the excesses perpetrated by the Red Guards. The implication is that Lin did.

A possible and reasonable explanation is that Mao grew distrustful of his heir during the Cultural Revolution, and that the parting of the ways between them was reached on the road to *rapprochement* with America and disagreement with Russia. Lin is believed to have opposed a deepening of the Sino-Russian rift and argued for a less aggressive posture towards Moscow while keeping up a cold front against Washington.

But Mao was unable to act directly or immediately against his 'close comrade in arms'. Lin could count on the support not only of many top commanders but of a considerable section of the people. Mao found himself unalterably opposed to a group of people whom he had encouraged and helped, and had frequently praised in public for their political-military work. It was an ironic situation which called for all the Chairman's guerrilla warfare expertise. So months of plots and counter-plots went by after the 1970 autumn meeting of the Party Congress. Lin was outmanoeuvred in all this intrigue, and a crisis point was reached when the only course open to him was to flee the country. The aircraft in which the escape attempt was made crashed in Mongolia. There is a theory that Lin and his fellow escapers tried to make the crew fly to Russia and that the crash was the result of a struggle or gun fight on the flight deck. The theory has also been advanced that the aircraft made a hurried departure and simply ran out of fuel, and the crash occurred as the crew attempted to make an emergency landing. The more likely explanation is that the Trident was intercepted and shot down by Chinese MiGs. Nevertheless, if this was so, it is surprising that they were able to penetrate Soviet-controlled air space with apparent ease.

Lin's sudden death and the resulting crisis threw the PLA into confusion, though not so great as might have been expected. There was, and still is, considerable unrest and dismay among the rank and file at the largely unexplained course of events which led to the abrupt removal not only of the defence chief but of many well-known and respected senior men, and which brought back close civilian control and supervision of the Army. The widespread feeling that the PLA had been badly used and unfairly judged, and was suffering for other people's undefined sins, did not result in any internal disorder. Just as it had adjusted after the 1959 purge, so did the PLA again after Lin's demise.

The soldiers are now being told that under Lin Piao the ideological and political mark was overstepped, that the theory of

Mao's genius was erroneous, that rather than teaching the people the PLA must now learn from the people. This must be all very confusing, and for the average soldier, who is as politically conscious as he is ordered to be, the about-turn and change into a more moderate pace has set him questioning. But the soldiers' minds have not turned to mutiny – a possibility which Mao had to take into account when organizing Lin's downfall. This demonstrates the basic stability of China's armed forces, no matter which political wind is prevailing.

Cheng Huan, an astute commentator on the PLA, summed up its mood and attitude when he wrote in the *Far East Economic Review*:

Despite ... bleak reports of Army-Party disunity, the danger of a deep rift seems to have passed the critical period, and the threatened Lin Piao tidal wave has been calmed to a comparative ripple by a Peking hierarchy more irritated than frightened. But then Mao's China has consistently proclaimed the need for rectification, adjustment and re-adjustment every few years. Even in the capitalist West, governments and people need to go through the rhythm of elections every few years.

The Lin incident completes a circle for the PLA. The 'Red versus expert' situation brought 'expert' Marshal Peng to the forefront, but he started on the slippery road down with his too great attachment to the Soviet Union and his nuclear advocacy, and 'Red' Lin plotted his own end when he began his programme of elevating Mao and his Thoughts to a ridiculous level. It is also instructive that both Marshals favoured an end to tension with the Soviet Union and closer co-operation with her. Both chose to argue a pro-Russian line at a time when Mao had started in an opposite direction; and in the end, the PLA, for all its strength and their careful husbanding of it, was unable to lift a finger to save them.

So what of the future? The likelihood is that so long as Mao and Chou En-lai hold the centre stage the PLA, under its new civilian guidance, will remain quiescent, content again to put 'the military art to the service of politics'.

But China is suffering a generation gap in the leadership, one as apparent in the Army as it is in politics. The men of the Long March and Yenan will not be around for ever and the question for the PLA is, will the youngsters who replace them be professionals or guerrillas? Perhaps more than any other race the Chinese study their own history and learn from it; and a cursory glance at the PLA's post-civil-war history shows that the men who have aspired to and gained a measure of political power through military leadership have been cast down after relatively short periods at the top.

Noting this, the new generation of military leaders will probably revert to professionalism. They are likely to play it safe, sticking to what they know and avoiding undue prominence in government. The disappearance of the old guard will almost certainly result in the ascendancy of the experts over the guerrillas with a consequent emphasis on the conventional martial arts over those of politics and the guerrilla. In short, the PLA will go back to what it does best – soldiering.

THE ARMY FOR THE 'SEVENTIES

A hundred victories in a hundred battles is
not the best of the best; the best of the
best is to subdue the enemy without having
to fight – *Chinese proverb*

Throughout the 'fifties, even during the Korean War, and for the
greater part of the last decade China's No. 1 enemy was the
Nationalist regime on the island fortress of Taiwan. The PLA
was deployed in strength along the eastern seaboard in order to
deter or repel any assault on the mainland from the belligerent
Kuomintang forces of Chiang Kai-shek, and at various times
preparations were made for an invasion of Taiwan although,
apart from a prolonged artillery bombardment of the off-shore
islands in 1958, they advanced little further than the planning and
preparatory training stage.

But with the deepening of the Sino-Russian quarrel and the
political isolation and military neutralizing of Taiwan, the High
Command has re-deployed many of its best divisions towards
the sensitive border areas in Manchuria, Inner Mongolia and
Sinkiang.

Until there is *rapprochement* with Moscow – and there are no
signs of this happening in the immediate future – Peking will
direct its main military effort to the development and improvement of her nuclear strike force while assigning much of her conventional capacity to threatened and vulnerable border zones. At
the same time the country is now in a state of semi-readiness to
fight a People's War should Russia attempt a deep penetration
after a pre-emptive nuclear attack.

But this 'alert' role on the rugged frontier areas is only one of a
number of formidable and varied duties which the three million
men of the PLA, the largest standing army in Asia, are expected
to perform and for which their seemingly vast numbers are no

more than sufficient. The Army still has to keep a watchful eye on Taiwan in case of any eleventh-hour adventures the government there might be tempted to try, and also on potential border trouble spots other than those under the shadow of Russia; at the same time it has to be prepared to go to the aid of the civil power, not only in a security role but to support work programmes on the land and construction and engineering tasks, even to help out in industry. Civilian-military co-operation plays an important role in the Chinese scheme of things and will continue to do so.

In areas such as Tibet and Sinkiang the PLA operates to some extent as an occupation army and has to be ready to deal with local disturbances, for these are troubled lands where the indigenous peoples might try to shake off China's hold should the opportunity ever present itself. As the years go by, however, the possibility of further troubles on the scale of those in Tibet in 1959 diminishes.

The demise of Lin Piao has relieved the PLA of much of its political work. This was both time-consuming and wasteful of manpower, and it did nothing to improve combat efficiency while probably loosening discipline. Efforts are being made to correct the balance, and some new system of ranks may yet be re-introduced.

The Army's distribution and deployment is spread unevenly over eleven Military Regions (see the organizational table) reflecting its many roles and duties. The Regions, with the exception of Sinkiang, are divided into Districts and they in turn are cut into sub-districts. The highest concentrations are, as noted above, on the periphery of the mainland, but much of the armour and some of the specialist formations are kept in the Peking area, which has good training grounds; they can also be readily put on show for political demonstrations of strength.

The commanders of these regions wield enormous power and, because of their semi-autonomous nature, it is possible for the men in charge of some of the bigger, more remote, regions to act very much on their own initiative, ignoring Peking directives when it suits them. The regional system is ideal for the waging of guerrilla war should China ever be invaded, but the disadvantage to the leadership is that it can produce unduly influential subordinates.

China also has a 'secret army' of some 20,000 men serving in northern Laos, and this force is causing considerable concern to a number of South-East Asian governments, particularly Thailand. In 1962 China and Laos signed an agreement for the construction of an all-weather highway in Houa Khong and Luang Prabang Provinces. With the outbreak of civil war the area through which the road was intended to run fell into the hands of the Communist Pathet Lao. Legally, the Chinese can claim the right to be there since in building the road they are fulfilling their side of the agreement. The artery, which is nearing completion, is described by American intelligence people as 'a motorable, all-weather surface, dual-lane highway', and it runs from Fuhsingchen in Yunnan to Muong Sai, deep in northern Laos, where it then branches east and west stretching to within twenty miles of the Thai border and in the other direction to Dien Bien Phu in North Vietnam.

The road is heavily defended by PLA anti-aircraft batteries which have shot down a number of reconnaissance or straying aircraft. At least fifteen patrol teams of the Royal Laotian Army have disappeared without trace in the vicinity of the road since 1970, and American and Laotian attempts to investigate it have now been largely abandoned. When the highway is completed it is likely that the PLA construction and air defence units will withdraw, but they will leave behind a route which can be used to reinforce all the Red guerrillas in Thailand, Burma and Laos, should China wish to do so. It will also assist Chinese troop movements should Peking ever decide to bring its border arguments with the Laotian Government to a military conclusion.

The PLA's total strength now stands at 150 divisions: 120 infantry, twenty artillery, five armoured, three cavalry and two airborne. An infantry division can number between twelve and fifteen thousand men while an armoured division contains some ten thousand. Three divisions, all infantry or a mix with other arms, usually make up an army, but there are no rigid formations and the individual strengths of the estimated thirty armies vary considerably.

After the Korean War, the PLA High Command was captivated by the idea of specialist forces, and airborne and Marine troops were introduced. These units are now elitist and service in them is regarded as a high honour and distinction.

The armoured divisions are equipped with T-62 light tanks, some T-60 amphibious tanks and a medium tank, the T-59, which is a copy of the Russian T-54. None of these tanks can compare with anything now used by Western, or even some Asian countries. They were out of date when China got them from Russia and the PLA has only been able to copy them without producing any greatly improved versions or successors. Also, the PLA has little battlefield experience of using armour and none at all in large-scale infantry–tank co-operation. It has to rely on Russian manuals and limited lessons from tactical field exercises.

In the 'sixties the infantry received a new family of automatic weapons, mortars and anti-tank guns, which have stood up to severe testing given them by the North Vietnamese and Viet Cong guerrillas. But much of the Army's heavy artillery is as obsolete as its tanks, although its anti-aircraft guns have proved effective in Vietnam and Laos.

The PLA has not been in action, except for border clashes, in the last decade and its battle readiness must vary enormously from division to division. It is equipped to fight a conventional war but has few weapons comparable with anything held by potential enemies, and how long the Chinese armaments industry could support the fighting forces in the event of the country becoming engaged in a protracted war is a matter for conjecture. It is doubtful if it could sustain the burden for very long particularly if the industrial plants came under air attack. With this in mind, the Government has recently made efforts to disperse some of its armament-producing factories which until 1969 were sited mainly in the vulnerable Manchurian area.

People's War is beyond doubt what the PLA is best qualified to wage. Guerrilla fighting is rooted in Chinese tradition, it suits the Chinese mentality and its principles have been given gospel authority by Mao and others of the Long March generation. Added to which the PLA's lack of sophisticated weapons forces the generals,

L

sometimes against their inclinations, to think and plan in guerrilla terms. The Peking Government is not offensive-minded, but even if it were the Army has neither the weaponry nor logistics support to engage in large-scale operations beyond its frontiers. Even within the mainland the PLA's mobility is restricted by lack of transport, both lorried and rail, and there is a chronic shortage of most types of armoured vehicles, particularly infantry carriers. The country's road and rail network is adequate in big city and industrial areas, but despite much effort and expenditure the communications system remains primitive in many areas and in some border regions is practically non-existent.

Military service is popular with the Chinese, and for those joining the Army it lasts for a minimum of two years. Those going into the Air Force serve three years while the Navy demands a four-year term. At any given time, China is estimated to have 100 million young men she can call upon for service.

Manpower is China's biggest military asset and as the years go by she is building a vast pool of reservists who carry out part-time training in the Militia after their regular engagements. The Militia has long been a bone of contention in military circles and it has not always proved popular with regular officers who have had to deal with it. During the Great Leap Forward the Militia was given a big boost. Under the slogan, 'Everyone a soldier', a campaign was launched to expand its ranks and duties. But as the Great Leap foundered, so the Militia sank back into obscurity, much to the relief of some PLA officers who had exhibited the usual professional dislike of the enthusiastic amateur.

In 1970, as a result of the tense situation between Peking and Moscow, fresh prominence was given to the Militia by the new provincial revolutionary committees, and in some Military Regions recruiting campaigns started. But there was argument over who should exercise control over the organization, the Party or the PLA. The latter tried to shun responsibility while the civilians claimed through the *People's Daily* that they had 'a thousand and one other tasks to carry out'. The Militia, now estimated at five million strong as compared to 200 million in 1959, is an important reserve force but clearly lacks leadership and direction. The PLA dislikes it for its political orientation, while the civilians are unable to run its military functions. Its problems remain unresolved, but its potential usefulness in the event of a national emergency or People's War is beyond question. When required, the leaders will emerge.

But while the Militia has been, until recently at least, in something of a limbo, the PLA's Production and Construction Corps, originally started in Sinkiang in the 'fifties, has shown remarkable growth in the last five years. A paramilitary organization, its strength is now estimated as at least equal to and possibly greater than the regular armed forces.

The Corps was founded to assist with the colonization of the border province, which meant that its members were expected to work on the land and be trained and ready to defend it. The Ministry of State Farms and Land Reclamation was originally responsible for the Corps, but after some factional fighting during the Cultural Revolution it was transferred to the PLA; the organization of it has since been tightened up and its military training intensified and improved. Units of the Corps are now based in Sinkiang, Inner Mongolia, Heilungkiang and Kwangtung. The decision to expand the Corps was probably taken during the 'war preparations' in the late 'sixties. Its military capacity is still limited, but it releases the 300,000 border security forces for more important and immediate work. The Production Corps seems to be very popular with the PLA High Command and field officers, and they certainly prefer it to the Militia. In wartime the Corps will probably be used for rear area duties, handling supply, labour and medical services and lines of communication duties. From what was essentially a local provincial unit, the Corps has developed into a national organization and the PLA's utility service.

In support of the regular Army, the border troops and the paramilitary organizations, China has a modest air force and navy. The Air Force has a strength of some 200,000 men and 3500 combat aircraft. After the rupture of relations with Russia the Air Force suffered some very lean years. It was short of jet fuel and spare parts, and front-line aircraft rapidly became obsolete by

Western standards. But in the last few years Chinese industry has overcome seemingly insuperable difficulties to provide the Air Force with at least one supersonic fighter, the Shenyang MiG 21 which has performed creditably against U.S. Phantoms in occasional clashes over the Gulf of Tonkin off North Vietnam, and it has proved popular with a buyer, the Pakistan Air Force.

Also in production is a twin-jet fighter, the F-9, which is believed to have a high performance and a long-range capability. In general, however, the Air Force lags far behind those belonging to industrialized countries, and it relies to a great extent on old MiG 19s and a bomber force of medium Tu-16s, both of which are at least a generation out of date.

An adequate transport fleet is also lacking, although in times of real emergency aircraft of various types and helicopters can be requisitioned from the Civil Air Bureau. China is trying to remedy her aircraft deficiencies in the transport field by buying from abroad.

For the past twenty years the Air Force's principal task has been to defend China from incursions from Taiwan and American spy planes. To this end an air defence system has been developed which incorporates an early warning-control radar, MiG interceptors and a few hundred surface-to-air missiles.

The Navy is even more limited than the Air Force. Its 160,000 personnel serve in three fleets, North Sea, East Sea and South Sea, and in a variety of vessels ranging from inshore patrol craft to submarines. China has no capital ships. In the future she is likely to concentrate on developing missile-carrying submarines, and possibly nuclear-powered submarines. But her marine technology is so far behind the other major powers that it is doubtful if she will ever catch up with them, even should she make the effort.

The role and duties of the PLA and its subsidiary formations often come up for public debate and discussion in China, but her nuclear progress is rarely mentioned. The taking of nuclear development out of politics and propaganda exercises is a deliberate act of policy. China also rarely emphasizes in her dialogues with other powers the destructiveness of nuclear weapons. This, again, is deliberate. She does not wish to highlight her own relative weakness and place herself in a position where she could be, or appear to be, blackmailed by the other nuclear powers. This does not mean that she is any less anxious than other nations to avoid a nuclear holocaust. She shares their concerns and no one in China, Mao included, still believes, if they ever really did, that nuclear weapons are 'paper tigers'. The Russian threat changed all that.

China's first nuclear device was exploded in 1964, since when she has carried out fourteen more tests. Her missile development has proceeded quite quickly and she now has deployed a group of medium-range ballistic missiles and a smaller clutch of inter-mediate-range ballistic missiles. They are housed in concrete silos or man-made caves in her mountainous western regions. It must be assumed that China will soon have ICBMs (inter-continental ballistic missiles) with nuclear warheads. Although she is not yet a major nuclear power, nevertheless, if she maintains her present rate of progress in this field, the next decade should see her a member of the big league. But even her present nuclear capacity adds a new factor or dimension to the problem of stability in Asia, even of global stability, and has to be reckoned with in any con-sideration of China's attitudes on world problems. Her nuclear arm is her silent but influential servant; though it gives her the strength to deter potential aggressors it is not sufficient to allow her any indulgence in military brinkmanship. But China has not the political will for offensive, expansionist action. She has enough internal problems to occupy her without looking abroad for any more; indeed, in her political–diplomatic–ideological war with Russia her aim is to find friends, not enemies.

Peking's oft-expressed theme has been that revolution is not for export, and this now assumes greater importance. Defence Minister Lin Piao alarmed the Western world in 1965 when he published his thesis entitled 'Long Live the Victory of People's War'. Its message was taken to be that China was prepared to meddle and cause mischief wherever the opportunity presented itself among the emergent and developing nations around the globe. This was not so. A closer reading of this document reveals the passage: 'If one does not operate by one's own efforts, does not independently ponder and solve the problems of the revolution in one's own country and does not rely on the strength of the masses, but leans wholly on foreign aid – even though this be aid from socialist countries which persist in revolution – no victory can be won, or be consolidated even if it be won.'

China's advice to others then is 'self-help', and it is advice which comes from her own experience. She may give moral support and encouragement through propaganda and publicity to the struggling revolutionary movements, but little else. Even where she has given she has received little in return. What China says and what China does about armed revolution and insurrection are two very different things. In this respect her behaviour is contradictory and it puzzles friends and enemies alike. To put it briefly: China tends to bluster. But there has been a marked reduction in the huffing and puffing since the 1969 Russian crisis.

Before leaving the subject there is one other factor which should be considered because it contributes to the China peril theme, the vision of hordes of olive green uniforms sweeping into Asia, swamping the area in an irresistible invasion tide: it is the role of the Overseas or Nanyang Chinese in the Peking scheme of things. For years these millions of Chinese have laboured under the suspicion that one day they may be used as some form of fifth column and advance units for an invasion from the mainland. This view was fostered by the Communist Emergency in Malaya in the 1950s and the Communist revolution in Indonesia in the 1960s. To think in these terms is to be grossly unfair to the Chinese who have fully identified with their countries of birth in South-East Asia. Far from encouraging subversion, Peking now earnestly encourages the Overseas Chinese to participate in the cultural and economic lives of their respective countries and where possible to assimilate with the peoples. The key to this attitude is that Peking looks at the Nanyang Chinese from an ideological not a racial standpoint. Her policy towards them is based on class and not race.

Goh Cheng-teik, who analysed China's approach on this question in a series of articles in the *Straits Times*, Malaysia, and the *Far East Economic Review*, neatly summed up the situation when he wrote: 'China is playing a global diplomatic game and has stakes in the world which are too large to be jeopardized by pan-Sinic adventurism in a small corner of the globe. As a result of the rivalry with Russia, China cannot afford to alienate the sympathy of the many native-led governments of South-East Asia for the sake of a few kith and kin whose way of life, in any case, looks suspiciously Kuomintang-like.' A good point. The Overseas Chinese, or at least their forebears, left China for lusher pastures, and many of them made good. In Peking's eyes the majority are capitalists, exploiters of labour, and she has turned her gaze from them.

But local suspicion of these Chinese remains. Malaysia's former Prime Minister, Tunku Abdul Rahman, once said that his country's frontier began at the Korean 38th Parallel and he spoke for many in 1968 when he declared that Red China's policy was to take over directly or indirectly all the South-East Asian countries. The important word here is 'indirectly'. But the danger to these countries comes not from an invasion by the PLA aided by an Overseas fifth column but in the actions of the various governments. If they reject the attempts of the indigenous Chinese to assimilate and identify with national aspirations, if they allow their resentment of Chinese economic power to lead to excessively repressive action while doing little or nothing for the poor Chinese (of whom there are many), and if they pay but lip service to their rights to equal opportunity, then there will be trouble. These Chinese may well look to Peking as a last resort and the leadership there could be tempted to revise the self-help policy. But this is a possibility likely to arise only in the distant future. For the moment China is pre-occupied with her economic and other development problems and her re-entry onto the world's stage, while quietly worrying about a political crisis after the death of Mao.

Her potential for the future is, of course, boundless. She has the manpower and resources, and when she finds the means to make full use of them, possibly with the help of Japan, she will be first among super-power equals.

What her military posture will be when that day dawns, a day when her nuclear capacity is fully developed and her economy

167

flourishing, a day without Mao Tse-tung, Chou En-lai and others of the Long March generation, none can say. But if China conducts herself in the future as she has in the past, and the likelihood is that her next leaders, whoever they may be, will see to it that she does so, then the world need not tremble.

Bibliography

1. GENERAL

Bloodworth, Dennis. *Chinese Looking Glass*. Secker & Warburg. London. 1967.

Elliott-Bateman, Michael. *Defeat in the East: The Mark of Mao Tse-tung on War*. Oxford University Press. London. 1967.

Fitzgerald, C. P. *The Birth of Communist China*. The Cresset Press. London. 1952. Penguin Books. Harmondsworth. 1964.

Franke, Wolfgang (ed.). *A Century of Chinese Revolution 1851–1949*. Translated by Stanley Rudman. Basil Blackwell. Oxford. 1970.

Mao Tse-tung. *Selected Military Writings*. Foreign Languages Press. Peking. 1963.

Mao Tse-tung. *Selected Works*. Lawrence & Wishart Ltd. London. 1954.

O'Ballance, Edgar. *The Red Army of China*. Faber & Faber. London. 1962.

Schram, Stuart. *Mao Tse-tung*. Penguin Books. Harmondsworth. 1966.

Snow, Edgar. *Red Star over China*. Gollancz. London. 1937.

Tuchman, Barbara W. *Sand against the Wind: Stilwell and the American Experience in China 1911–1945*. Macmillan. New York. 1971.

Wilson, Dick. *A Quarter of Mankind: an anatomy of China today*. Weidenfeld & Nicolson. London. 1966.

Wilson, Dick. *Asia Awakes: a Continent in transition*. Weidenfeld & Nicolson. London. 1970.

United States-China Relations: a strategy for the future (Hearings before the sub-committee on Asian and Pacific Affairs of the Committee on Foreign Affairs, House of Representatives) Washington, D.C. 1970.

169

Bibliography

2. THE CAMPAIGN IN TIBET 1950–1960

Chanyaka Sen (ed.). *Tibet Disappears: a documentary history of Tibet's international status, the Great Rebellion and its aftermath.* Asia Publishing House. Bombay. 1960.

Dalai Lama XIV (Nga-wang Lop-sang Ten-sin Gya-tso). *My Land and My People.* Edited by David Howarth. Weidenfeld & Nicolson. London. 1962.

Moraes, Frank. *The Revolt in Tibet.* Macmillan. New York. 1960.

Patterson, George N. *Tibet in Revolt.* Faber & Faber. London. 1960.

Richardson, H. E. *Tibet and its History.* Oxford University Press. Oxford. 1962.

Thubten Jigme Norbu. *Tibet is my Country*: as told to Heinrich Farrer. Translated from the German by Edward FitzGerald. Rupert Hart-Davis. London. 1960.

Concerning the Question of Tibet. Foreign Languages Press. Peking. 1959.

The Question of Tibet and the Rule of Law. International Commission of Jurists. Geneva. 1959.

3. THE KOREAN WAR 1950–1953

Carew, Tim. *Korea: The Commonwealth at War.* Cassell & Co. Ltd. London. 1967.

Higgins, Trumbull. *Korea and the Fall of MacArthur.* Oxford University Press. New York. 1960.

Leckie, Robert. *The Korean War.* Pall Mall Press. London. 1963.

Rees, David. *Korea: The Limited War.* Macmillan. London/New York. 1964.

Rigg, Robert B. *Red China's Fighting Hordes.* Military Service Publishing Company, Harrisburg, Pa. 1952.

4. WAR WITH INDIA 1962

Bhargava, G. S. *The Battle of NEFA: The Undeclared War.* Allied Publishers. Bombay. 1964.

Dalvi, Brigadier J. P. *Himalayan Blunder: The Curtain raiser to the Sino-Indian War of 1962.* Thacker & Co. Bombay. 1969.

Fisher, Margaret W., Rose, Leo E., Huttenback, Robert A. *Himalayan Battleground: Sino-Indian Rivalry in Ladakh.* Pall Mall Press. London. 1963.

170

Kaul, Lieut.-General B. M. *The Untold Story*. Allied Publishers. Bombay. 1967.

Mankekar, D. R. *The Guilty Men of 1962*. Tulsi Shah Enterprises. Bombay. 1968.

Maxwell, Neville. *India's China War*. Jonathan Cape. London. Jaico Publishing House. Bombay. 1970.

Sharma, Surya P. *The Chinese Recourse to Force against India*. External Publicity Division of the Government of India. 1966.

Woodman, Dorothy. *Himalayan Frontiers: a political review of British, Chinese, Indian and Russian rivalries*. Barrie & Rockcliff. London. 1969.

The Sino-Indian Boundary Question. Foreign Languages Press. Peking. 1962.

5. CONFRONTATION WITH RUSSIA 1969–1973

Beloff, Max. *Soviet Policy in the Far East, 1944–1951*. Oxford University Press. London. 1953.

Crankshaw, Edward. *The New Cold War: Moscow v. Peking*. Penguin Books. Harmondsworth. 1963.

Salisbury, Harrison. *War between Russia and China*. Bantam Books (expanded edition). 1971.

6. THE ARMY AND POLITICS

Joffe, Ellis. 'The Chinese Army in the Cultural Revolution: the politics of intervention.' *Current Scene*, viii (1970), no. 18.

Johnson, Chalmers. 'Lin Piao's Army and its Role in Chinese Society.' *Current Scene*, iv (1966), no. 13.

'Lin Piao: a political profile.' *Current Scene*, vii (1969), no. 5.

'Lin Piao and the Cultural Revolution.' *Current Scene*, viii (1970), no. 14.

Whitson, William W. (ed.). *The Military and Political Power in China in the 1970s*. Praeger. New York. 1972.

7. JOURNALS AND PERIODICALS

Bulletin of the Institute for the study of U.S.S.R.
China Quarterly.
Far Eastern Economic Review.
Journal of the Royal United Services Institute for Defence Studies.
The Military Balance. Institute of Strategic Studies.

Bibliography

8. NEWSPAPERS

Nanyang Siang Pau. Singapore.
South China Morning Post. Hong Kong.
Straits Times. Singapore/Kuala Lumpur.

9. HANDBOOKS

Asia Handbook. Edited by Guy Wint. Penguin Books (revised edition).
   Harmondsworth. 1969.
China Yearbook 1967–1968. China Publishing Co. Taipei, Taiwan.

Index

Acheson, Dean, 70
Aigun, Treaty of, 122
Air Force, 163–4
Aksai Chin, 93, 96
Alexander, General, 19
Amdo, 62
Amdos, 52; revolt of, 57–62
Amur, River, 116, 122, 123, 127, 131, 134, 140
Argun River, 121, 140
Assam, 110

Babanski, Sergeant Y., 115–16
Bailey Trail, 107
'Bandit' extermination, 33–4
Bangladesh, 110
Bhutan, 55, 105
Bloodworth, Dennis, 22–3, 88
Bomdi La, 106–9
Bradley, General, on MacArthur, 80
Brezhnev, Leonid, 136
Bubenin, Lieutenant V., 116
Burma, 19, 20, 160
Burma Road, 37

Canton, 32
Chaku, 109
Chamdo, 54; capture of, 51–2
Chang Ching-wu, General, 55
Chang Kuo-hua, General, 55, 61, 62–4
Chang Tang, 55
Chen Pao Island, 112–22, 134
Cheng Huan, 156
Chengtu, 63–4
Chiang Ching, 151–2
Chiang Kai-shek, 19–20, 21, 28–42, 126, 158; in Taiwan, 42, 47; U.S. support for, 72

Chinese Looking Glass, 23, 88
Choisin Reservoir, 67
Chou En-lai, 31–2, 73–4, 130–31, 154, 156, 168
Chu Teh, 28–30, 33, 143, 144
Chungking, 37
Civil War, 20, 28–42, 47, 50
Commission on River Navigation, 129–30
Common Market, 139
Cultural Revolution, 26, 127, 142, 151–5, 163; in Tibet, 62–3
Czechoslovakia, invasion of, 119–20

Dalai Lama, 46, 54–5, 58–9, 96; flees to India, 59, 60; in Yatung, 54; on Chinese in Tibet, 62
'Dalforce', 19
Dalvi, Brigadier, 101
Damansky Island, 112–22, 134
Davies, Derek, 26n.
Defeat in the East, 89
Dhola, 98
Dien Bien Phu, 160
Dirang Dzong, 106–8

Eisenhower, President, 83
Elliott-Bateman, Michael, on the PLA, 89

Far East Economic Review, 156, 166–7
First World War, 23, 81–2, 85
Flanders, 23
Fuhsingchen, 160

Gandhi, Mahatma, 98
Gartok, 93
Genghis Khan, 126
Goh Cheng-teik, 166–7

Index

Goldinsky Island, 120
Goloks, 52; revolt of, 57–62
Gongbo, 60
Great Leap Forward, 142, 146, 149, 151, 162
Gun Hsi, 115

Han River, 71
Hanoi, 130–31
Hiroshima, bombing of, 38
Ho Chi Minh, 49; death of, 130; testament of, 130–31
Hong Kong, 19
Houa Khong, 160
Hsinhua, 129–30
Huai Hai, Battle of, 42

Inchon landings, 67, 73, 79
India, 92–111; and the Korean War, 97; China's war aims in, 103
Indian Army, 92–111
India's China War, 103
Indo-China, 70; French in, 45
Indo-Chinese War, 92–111; casualties, 110; end of, 110; foreign aid to India, 105; Russia and, 138; Third World and, 105
Indonesia, Communist revolution, 166

Japan, defeat of, 38

Kaesong, 83
Kaohsing, 34
Kaul, General B. M., 99–101, 106, 108–9
Kazakhstan, 137
Kennedy, President, 70
Khabarovsk, 112, 130
Kham, 60, 61, 62
Khambas, 52–4; revolt of, 57–62
Khrushchev and nuclear aid, 145
Kiangsi Soviet, 32–5
Korea, 65–91; peace talks, 83–4; U.N. forces in, 65–91
Korean War, 43, 45, 49, 53, 65–91, 97, 142, 158, 161; casualties in, 82, 83; effects of on China, 85–91; end of, 84
Kosygin in Peking, 131ff.
Kovalyov, Private, 116
Kuomintang, 28–42, 143, 158
Kwangtung, 29

Ladakh, 92–3, 104, 110

Lamaism, Chinese attempt to destroy, 62
Laos, 160; Chinese 'secret army' in, 160
Lenin, 122
Lhasa, 51, 54, 58, 61, 64
Lhoka, 59–60
Liberation Army Daily, 127–8
Lin Piao, 29–30, 68, 128, 147–56, 165; death of, 137, 141, 153, 155, 159; in Korea, 76–8
Lo Jui-ching, 148, 149
Long March, 34–6, 142, 148, 168; end of, 36
Luang Prabang, 160

MacArthur, General, 83; dismissal of, 79–80; in Korea, 65–80
Malaya, 19, 45, 166–7
Malik, Jacob, 82
Manchuria, 34, 35, 38, 41, 74, 76, 80, 158; Russian occupation of, 125–6
Mao Tse-tung, 23–7, 29–30, 32–42, 63, 70, 75, 84, 102, 118, 126, 127–8, 131, 167, 168; and Korean War, 70–71; and PLA, 141–2, 144–57; and PLA purge, 141; and Tibet, 46–9; in Moscow, 46; meets Tibetan delegation, 54–5; on guerrilla warfare, 24–5, 27; on nuclear weapons, 165
Marco Polo Bridge, 37
Matsu, attack on, 145, 158
Matveev, G. V., 138
Maxwell, Neville, 103
McMahon Line, 93–5, 98, 101, 106
Menon, Krishna, 97
Military Regions, 159
Militia, 162–3
Mongolia, 70, 125, 136, 153, 155, 158
Mukden, surrender of, 42
Muong Sai, 160

Nagasaki, bombing of, 38
Nagorny, Lieut.-Col. V., 115–16
Namka Chu River, 103
Nanchang, 28, 29
Nanyang Chinese, 166–7
Nationalist Army, 19–20, 23, 28–42; final defeat of, 42
Navy, 163, 164
NEFA, 92ff., 99–111
Nehru, Jawaharlal, 95–8, 105, 106; and Tibet, 54

Nepal, 55
Nerchinsk, Treaty of, 121
Ngabon Ngawang Jigme, 51, 54
North Vietnam, 130–31, 160
Nuclear power, 145, 147; weapons, 164–5

'Old Hundred Names', 22–3, 24, 27
Operation Leghorn, 99–103
Overseas Chinese, 166–7

Pamir Plateau, 135
Panchen Lama, 54–5; as Chinese puppet, 55
Panmunjom, 83
Pathet Lao, 160
Peking, capture of, 42; Treaty of, 122, 123
Peng Teh-huai, 144, 145–7, 149; in Korea, 78–81, 87, 90
People's Daily, 162
People's Republic established, 42
People's War, 144
PLA, *passim*; and politics, 141–57; birth of, 28; casualties in Tibet, 54; deployment of, 159–60; future of, 158–68; in India, 92–111; in Korea, 49, 65–91; in Laos, 160; in Manchuria, 41–2, 74; in Tibet, 43–64; on Russian frontier, 158; Political Department, 148; present strength and equipment, 160–62; reforms, 148; road-building in Tibet, 56
Politburo, 141–57
Prichkin, Lieut.-Col. B., 115–16
Problems of the Far East, 138
Pusan, 71, 72
PVA, formation of, 76; in Korea, 76–91; withdraws from Korea, 84

Quemoy, 48; attack on, 145, 158

Red Guards, 62–3, 151–2
Rhee, Dr Syngman, 69
Ridgway, General, 69n., 86
ROK units, 71
Royal Laotian Army, 160
Rupa, 109
Russia and the Korean War, 69–91; forces in Korea, 69
Russian Military Mission, 143
Russo-Chinese Confrontation, 112–40; Peking talks, 131–5
Russo-Japanese War, 122

St Petersburg Treaty, 123
Se La, 104–8
Second World War, 19, 23, 37
Seoul, fall of, 71, 78
17-Point Agreement, 54–5
Shanghai, 29; massacre in, 31–2
Shensi, 35f.
Sian Incident, 36–7
Siberia, 136
Sikang, 50, 55
Sikkim, 55
Simla Agreement, 45–6, 48
Singh, Brigadeer Gurbax, 108–9
Sinkiang, 48, 49, 55, 58, 70, 93, 123, 124, 140, 158, 159
Sino-Japanese War, 20, 23, 36–8
Sino-Russian Confrontation, 112–40; Peking talks, 131–5
Sino-Russian quarrel, 76, 121–6
South Korean Army, 65–91
Stalin, 126; and Korea, 70, 74; death of, 83–4; supplies arms to China, 74
Stilwell, 'Vinegar Joe', 20
Straits Times, 166–7
Strelnikov, Lidia, 116
Strelnikov, Lieutenant I., 115, 117–18
Sun Yat-sen, 30, 31
Sung, Kim Il, 69
Szechwan, 49–50, 53, 63–4

Taejon, 71
Taiping Rebellion, 30
Taiwan, 37, 47, 71, 72, 143, 158, 159; Intelligence Service, 153–4; proposed invasion of, 47, 49
Tawang Tract, 95, 105
Tensoon Magar, 57–62
Thag La Ridge, 98–106
Thailand, 160
Thoughts of Mao, 149, 154
Tibet, 159; air attacks on, 58, 61; and the U.N., 54, 60–61; Chinese claims on, 45; Chinese coercion in, 56–7; Chinese 'colonists' in, 57, 63; invasion of, 43–64; propaganda campaign in, 50–51; refugees from, 60; road-building in, 50; tribal uprising in, 57–62; world-opinion on, 60–61
Tibet–Sikang highway, 56
Tibetan Army, 51–2
Trans-Siberian Railway, 112–13
Truman, President, 68, 79–80; on Taiwan, 72

Index

Tsedang, 60
Tsinghai, 50, 58; highway, 56
Tunku Abdul Rahman, 167

U.N. and Korea, 65–91
U.S.A. and the Civil War, 38, 41;
    forces in Korea, 65–91; 7th Fleet,
    72–3
Ussuri River, 112–22, 123, 134, 140

Viet Minh, 49

Vietnam War, 128, 149
Vladivostok, 112–13

Wake Island, 74
War in Korea, The, 69n.

Yalu River, 65ff., 73, 74, 76, 80,
    86
Yatung, 54
Yenan, 35–6, 141
Yunnan, 49, 160